IRAQ

AZERBAIJAN

Caspian Sea

TURKEY

N
W   E
S

SYRIA

Al Mawşil

Arbīl

M
E
S
O
P
O
T
A
M
I
A

Hamrīn Range

Tigris River

IRAN

Euphrates River

Tharthār L.

Baghdad

SYRIAN DESERT

Razzāzah L.

JORDAN

IRAQ

Karbalā'

Al Hillah

An Najaf

Al 'Amārah

An Nāşirīyah

Al Başrah

Persian Gulf

KUWAIT

Sahra Al Ḩijārah

SAUDI ARABIA

0   50   100 Miles
0   50   100 Kilometers
Albers Conic Equal-Area Projection

38N

36N

34N

32N

30N

28N

26N

40E   42E   44E   46E   48E

IRAQ

Bill and Dorcas Thompson

MC MASON CREST
PHILADELPHIA

Mason Crest
450 Parkway Drive, Suite D
Broomall, PA 19008
www.masoncrest.com

Printed and bound in the United States of America.

CPSIA Compliance Information: Batch #MNMME2016.
For further information, contact Mason Crest at 1-866-MCP-Book.

3 5 7 9 8 6 4 2

Library of Congress Cataloging-in-Publication Data
        on file at the Library of Congress

            ISBN: 978-1-4222-3442-6 (hc)
            ISBN: 978-1-4222-8435-3 (ebook)

Major Nations of the Modern Middle East series ISBN: 978-1-4222-3438-9

TABLE OF CONTENTS

MAJOR NATIONS OF THE MODERN MIDDLE EAST

Afghanistan

Egypt

Iran

Iraq

Israel

Jordan

The Kurds

Lebanon

Pakistan

The Palestinians

Saudi Arabia

Syria

Turkey

KEY ICONS TO LOOK FOR:

 Words to Understand: These words with their easy-to-understand definitions will increase the reader's understanding of the text, while building vocabulary skills.

 Sidebars: This boxed material within the main text allows readers to build knowledge, gain insights, explore possibilities, and broaden their perspectives by weaving together additional information to provide realistic and holistic perspectives.

 Research Projects: Readers are pointed toward areas of further inquiry connected to each chapter. Suggestions are provided for projects that encourage deeper research and analysis.

 Text-Dependent Questions: These questions send the reader back to the text for more careful attention to the evidence presented there.

 Series Glossary of Key Terms: This back-of-the book glossary contains terminology used throughout this series. Words found here increase the reader's ability to read and comprehend higher-level books and articles in this field.

Introduction

by Camille Pecastaing, Ph.D.

O il shocks, wars, terrorism, nuclear proliferation, military and autocratic regimes, ethnic and religious violence, riots and revolutions are the most frequent headlines that draw attention to the Middle East. The region is also identified with Islam, often in unflattering terms. The creed is seen as intolerant and illiberal, oppressive of women and minorities. There are concerns that violence is not only endemic in the region, but also follows migrants overseas. All clichés contain a dose of truth, but that truth needs to be placed in its proper context. The turbulences visited upon the Middle East that grab the headlines are only the symptoms of a deep social phenomenon: the demographic transition. This transition happens once in the life of a society. It is the transition from the agrarian to the industrial age, from rural to urban life, from illiteracy to mass education, all of which supported by massive population growth. It is this transition that fueled the recent development of East Asia, leading to rapid social and economic modernization and to some form of democratization there. It is the same transition that, back in the 19th century, inspired nationalism and socialism in Europe, and that saw the excesses of imperialism, fascism, and Marxist-Leninism. The demographic transition is a period of high risks and great opportunities, and the challenge for the Middle East is to fall on the right side of the sword.

In 1950, the population of the Middle East was about 100 million; it passed 250 million in 1990. Today it exceeds 400 million, to reach about 700 million by 2050. The growth of urbanization is rapid, and concentrated on the coasts and along the few rivers. 1950 Cairo, with an estimated population of 2.5 million, grew into Greater Cairo, a metropolis of about 18 million people. In the same period, Istanbul went from one to 14 million. This expanding populace was bound to test the social system, but regimes were unwilling to take chances with the private sector, reserving for the state a prominent place in the economy. That model failed, population grew faster than the economy, and stress fractures already appeared in the 1970s, with recurrent riots following IMF adjustment programs and the emergence of radical Islamist movements. Against a backdrop of military coups and social unrest, regimes consolidated their rule by subsidizing basic commodities, building up patronage networks (with massive under-employment in a non-productive public sector), and cementing autocratic practices. Decades of continuity in political elites between 1970 and 2010 gave the impression that they had succeeded. The Arab spring shattered that illusion.

The Arab spring exposed a paradox that the Middle East was both one, yet also diverse. Arab unity was apparent in the contagion: societies inspired other societies in a revolutionary wave that engulfed the region yet remained exclusive to it. The rebellious youth was the same; it watched the same footage on al Jazeera and turned to the same online social networks. The claims were the same: less corruption, less police abuse, better standards of living, and off with the tyrants. In some cases, the struggle was one: Syria became a global battlefield, calling young fighters from all around the region to a common cause. But there were differences in the way states fared during the Arab spring. Some escaped unscathed; some got by with a burst of public spending or a sprinkling of democratic reforms, and others yet collapsed into civil wars. The differential resilience of the regimes owes to both the strength and cohesiveness of the repressive apparatus, and the depth of the fiscal cushion they could tap into to buy social peace. Yemen, with a GDP per capita of $4000 and Qatar, at $94,000, are not the same animal. It also became apparent that, despite shared frustrations and a common cause, protesters and insurgents were extremely diverse.

Some embraced free-market capitalism, while others clamored for state welfare to provide immediate improvements to their standards of living. Some thought in terms of country, while other questioned that idea. The day after the Arab spring, everyone looked to democracy for solutions, but few were prepared to invest in the grind of democratic politics. It also quickly became obvious that the competition inherent in democratic life would tear at the social fabric. The few experiments with free elections exposed the formidable polarization between Islamists and non-Islamists. Those modern cleavages paralleled ancient but pregnant divisions. Under the Ottoman Millet system, ethnic and sectarian communities had for centuries coexisted in relative, self-governed segregation. Those communities remained a primary feature of social life, and in a dense, urbanized environment, fractures between Christians and Muslims, Shi'as and Sunnis, Arabs and Berbers, Turks and Kurds were combustible. Autocracy had kept the genie of divisiveness in the bottle. Democracy unleashed it.

This does not mean democracy has to forever elude the region, but that in countries where the state concentrates both political and economic power, elections are a polarizing zero-sum game—even more so when public patronage has to be cut back because of chronic budget deficits. The solution is to bring some distance between the state and the national economy. If all goes well, a growing private sector would absorb the youth, and generate taxes to balance state budgets. For that, the Middle East needs just enough democracy to mitigate endemic corruption, to protect citizens from abuse and extortion, and to allow greater transparency over public finances and over licensing to crony privateers.

Better governance is necessary but no sufficient. The region still needs to figure out a developmental model and find its niche in the global economy. Unfortunately, the timing is not favorable. Mature economies are slow growing, and emerging markets in Asia and Africa are generally more competitive than the Middle East. To succeed, the region has to leverage its assets, starting with its geographic location between Europe, Africa, and Asia. Regional businesses and governments are looking to anchor themselves in south-south relationships. They see the potential clientele of hundreds of millions in Africa and South Asia reaching middle class status, many of whom Muslim. The Middle East can also count on its vast sources of energy, and on the capital accumulated during years of high oil prices. Financial investments in specific sectors, like transport, have already made local companies like Emirates Airlines and DP World global players.

With the exception of Turkey and Israel, the weakness is human capital, which is either unproductive for lack of adequate education, or uncompetitive, because wage expectations in the region are relatively higher than in other emerging economies. The richer Arab countries have worked around the problem by importing low-skilled foreign labor—immigrants who notoriously toil for little pay and even less protection. In parallel, they have made massive investments in higher education, so that the productivity of their native workforce eventually reaches the compensations they expect. For lack of capital, the poorer Arab countries could not follow that route. Faced with low capitalization, sticky wages and high unemployment, they have instead allowed a shadow economy to grow. The arrangement keeps people employed, if at low levels of productivity, and in a manner that brings no tax revenue to the state.

Overall, the commerce of the region with the rest of the world is unhealthy. Oil exporters tend to be one-product economies highly vulnerable to fluctuations in global prices. Labor-rich countries depend too much on remittances from workers in the European Union and the oil-producing countries of the Gulf. Some of the excess labor has found employment in the jihadist sector, a high-risk but up and coming industry which pays decent salaries. For the poorer states of the region, jihadists are the ticket to foreign strategic rent. The Middle East got a taste for it in the early days of the Cold War, when either superpower provided aid to those who declared themselves in their camp. Since then, foreign strategic rent has come in many forms: direct military aid, preferential trade agreements, loan guarantees, financial assistance, or aid programs to cater to refugee populations. Rent never amounts to more than a few percentage points of GDP, but it is often enough to keep entrenched regimes in power. Dysfunction becomes self-perpetuating: pirates and jihadists, famine and refugees, all bear promises of aid to come from concerned distant powers. Reforms lose their urgency.

Turkey and Israel have a head start on the path to modernization and economic maturity, but they are, like the rest of the Middle East, consumed in high stakes politics that hinder their democratic life. Rather than being models that would lift others, they are virtually outliers disconnected from the rest of the region. The clock is ticking for the Middle East. The window of opportunity from the demographic transition will eventually close. Fertility is already dropping, and as the current youth bulge ages it will become a burden on the economy. The outlook for capital is also bleak. Oil is already running out for the smaller producers, all the while global prices are pushed downwards by the exploitation of new sources. The Middle East has a real possibility to break the patterns of the past, but the present is when the transition should occur.

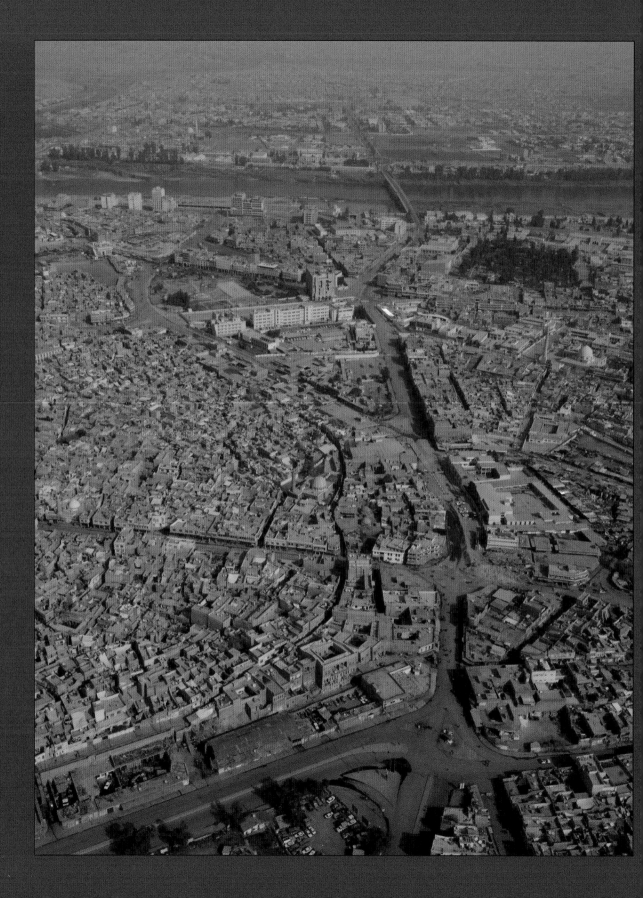

An aerial view of Mosul, one of Iraq's largest cities, which was captured in June 2014 by a terrorist organization calling itself the Islamic State. Iraq has not been stable or peaceful since the 2003 invasion by an international coalition led the United States to topple dictator Saddam Hussein. Since 2011, religious and ethnic tensions among Iraqis have been made worse by the ongoing civil war in neighboring Syria and the rise of the Islamic State.

IRAQ'S PLACE IN THE WORLD

During the first six months of 2014, an organization calling itself the Islamic State of Iraq and the Levant (ISIL) launched a major offensive against the government of Iraq. ISIL militias, armed with weapons from the civil war in neighboring Syria, captured numerous villages and cities in northern Iraq from government forces. These included the Sunni Muslim strongholds of Fallujah and Ramadi, as well as the city of Mosul, with more than a million inhabitants. On June 29, 2014, ISIL's leaders declared that the group had established a caliphate, based in Iraq, that would henceforth have religious, political, and military authority over all Muslims throughout the world.

The threat of ISIL worried Iraq's neighbors, such as Saudi Arabia and Jordan, who feared that the violence would spill over into their borders. In August 2014, the United States decided to intervene in the conflict in order to prevent ISIL from carrying out a program of ***genocide*** against the Kurdish people of northern

13

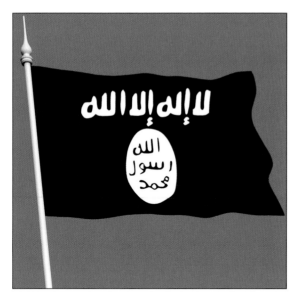

The flag of the Islamic State of Iraq and the Levant is a black banner that includes the shahada, an important Muslim statement of belief. The circle design is said to be the "seal of Muhammad," the chief prophet of Islam. Other Islamist terror organizations have adopted a black banner as well.

Iraq, as well as to support the Iraqi government, which America had helped bring to power less than a decade earlier. The U.S. provided humanitarian aid to the Kurds, who were taking refuge from ISIL on Mount Sinjar, and launched airstrikes against ISIL positions.

Despite the U.S. intervention, in October 2014 some 10,000 ISIL troops nearly reached Baghdad, the capital city of Iraq, before finally being halted by the Iraqi Army, supported by U.S. airstrikes.

The ISIL threat brought international attention to Iraq, a country that for many years has seemed to be on the verge of disintegration. Iraq as an independent political entity, or nation-state, was formed after the end of World War I. The country's borders

Words to Understand in This Chapter

caliph—an Arabic word meaning "successor," and traditionally denoting the successor to Muhammad as head of the Islamic community.

genocide—the deliberate killing of a large group of people, especially those of a particular ethnic group or nation.

industrialized—having many manufacturing and industrial businesses.

Kurdish militias, known as peshmerga, have defended cities like Kirkuk and Erbil from the Islamic State invasion when the Arab-dominated Iraqi Army abandoned their posts. That has led to concerns that the Kurdistan region may break away from Iraq and form an independent state—a prospect that would be unpalatable to neighboring Turkey, which has its own restive Kurdish population.

include three groups of people who have often been at odds throughout their history: Shiite Muslims, Sunni Muslims, and Kurds.

The rise of ISIL provides both a threat and an opportunity to the Kurds. As ISIL forces captured Iraqi cities and villages during 2014, the soldiers of the Iraqi Army fled, setting off a military collapse through the region. Kurdish fighters, known as peshmerga, recovered from the initial attack. By engaging with ISIL, they managed to prevent the country from disintegrating completely. But in the process the Kurds gained control of lands that had ben claimed by

Iraqis have begun to develop some of the elements of a successful democratic society, such as elections that are free and fair and an opportunity for citizens to question government leaders and be involved in politics. However, the ongoing violence threatens to tear the country apart.

both Iraqi Kurdistan and the government in Baghdad. As the fighting continued, the leader of Kurdistan's regional government, Masoud Barzani, told the local parliament to begin preparing for a plebiscite on gaining independence from Iraq.

To many people in the West, the brutal dictatorship of Saddam Hussein, from 1979 until his overthrow in April 2003, and the years of internecine violence that followed his overthrow are the major reference points for Iraq. Yet the region has a history that is long and glorious. Mesopotamia, the land between the Tigris and Euphrates Rivers in modern-day Iraq, is known as the "cradle of civilization" because the earliest known human civilization was established here more than 5,500 years ago. During the high point of the Arab Islamic civilization, from the 8th to the 13th centuries CE, Baghdad was the seat of the Muslim **caliphs**, and thus the center of the Islamic world. Iraq was one of the first Arab nations to gain independence in the 20th century, and until the 1991 Gulf War it was considered an important Arab cultural center. The country is also important to the **industrialized** countries of the West because of its large reserves of oil. Iraq's known petroleum reserves are among the largest in the world, and the country has the potential to be a major exporter of oil, although significant upgrades to the national infrastructure are needed to maximize Iraq's capacity.

The future of Iraq remains uncertain. It may take years, or even decades, for Iraq to achieve stability and prosperity. But whatever happens in the Middle East over the next few years, it is likely that Iraq—with its vast oil reserves, its large population, and its rich cultural heritage—will play an important role.

 Text-Dependent Questions

1. What major Iraqi city did ISIL capture in June 2014?
2. What are the three major ethnic or religious groups in Iraq?
3. Who was dictator of Iraq from 1979 until his overthrow in 2003?

 Research Project

There are many different definitions of what terrorism is. Each person in your class should research recent news items to find examples of terrorist acts. Discuss these examples. Keeping in mind the contexts of the attacks, as well as the ideologies of the groups that committed them, what are the common elements, and how is each one different? Ask members of the group to try to define terrorism, and discuss the pros and cons of each definition. Consider the following questions: What differentiates terrorists from warriors, freedom fighters, or patriots? Is any attack on civilians a terrorist act? When governments bomb cities, is it terrorism?

View of the Euphrates River as it passes through the village of Hit. One of Iraq's two major rivers, the Euphrates originates in Turkey.

The Land

I raq lies on the northern shore of the Arabian Gulf, more commonly known as the Persian Gulf among non-Arabs. Its small segment of coastline is situated between the much longer shorelines of Iran to its east and Kuwait to its south.

Iraq possesses a land area of some 168,754 square miles (437,072 square kilometers), making it slightly more than twice the size of Idaho. If Iraq were placed over the eastern part of the United States, its southern edge would rest at Raleigh, North Carolina, and its northern edge in Lake Ontario. The width of Iraq would stretch from Washington, D.C., in the east to Indianapolis, Indiana, in the west.

Iraq is surrounded by six countries, four of which are, like Iraq, populated by Arabs. Kuwait lies to the southeast of Iraq. To the south and southwest is the larger country of Saudi Arabia. Jordan, to the west of Iraq, shares a 113-mile (181-km) border. To the northwest is Syria, which borders Iraq for 376 miles (605 km). The two non-Arab countries that border Iraq are Turkey, which lies to the north, and Iran, to the east.

THE RIVERS

Centuries before the name "Iraq" was used, the Greeks called the area between the Tigris and Euphrates Rivers "Mesopotamia," which means "between the rivers." It is along these rivers—especially at Baghdad and to the south—where most of Iraq's people have settled and where the country's heaviest industries have developed. From very early times, an *irrigation* system was developed that allowed agriculture to expand into the land between the two rivers. Thus the rivers have made the land fertile, helping people fortunate enough to live there to prosper.

The Tigris River has its source in the mountains of eastern Turkey. It enters Iraq in the far north and zigzags southeast through the country for 881 miles (1,418 km). After flowing through Baghdad, Iraq's capital city, the Tigris continues southeast to the town of Al Qurnah, where it meets the Euphrates River. The united rivers then become the Shatt al Arab, which flows south for about 100 miles (161 km) before entering the Persian Gulf. For much of this distance the river marks Iraq's southeastern border with Iran.

For centuries, the Tigris River flooded in late winter and early

 Words to Understand in This Chapter

alluvial—related to river-deposited materials like silt laid down on floodplains and deltas.
irrigation—to supply water to farmland by artificial means, such as diverting it from a river or other water source, or by spraying it onto the land.
wadi—an dry streambed that may flood after heavy rains.

Iraq's terrain consists mostly of low-lying plains and desert. The north and northeast are mountainous; marshes cover parts of the southeast, along the border with Iran.

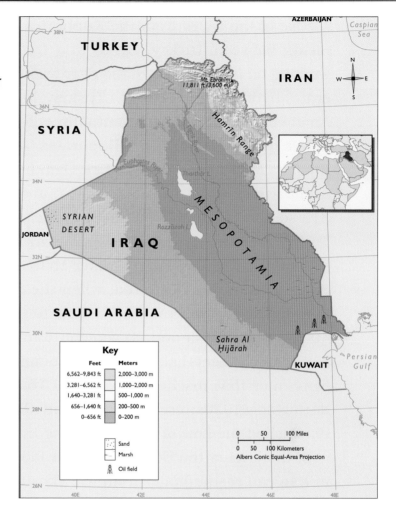

spring because of rains in the north. However, in the 1950s the Samarra Dam was built in central Iraq. When the river level is particularly high, the dam helps divert water into the Tharthar Reservoir, where it can be stored for later use.

Like the Tigris, the Euphrates River also originates in Turkey. It flows first through Syria and then enters Iraq in the northwest, running through the country for 743 miles (1,196 km). The Euphrates flows along a channel that is roughly parallel to that of the Tigris. As they flow through Iraq, the two rivers are between 25 and 100 miles (40 and 161 km) apart. Eventually, the Euphrates joins the Tigris at Al Qurnah.

Use of the water from the Euphrates River has led to disagreements between Turkey, Syria, and Iraq. All three countries are working on projects to use the river water to irrigate crops and generate hydroelectric power. Turkey has begun the Southeast Anatolia Project, which eventually will create 22 dams and 19 power plants where the Euphrates cascades down from the Anatolia Mountains. The Atatürk Dam in Turkey, one of the largest in the world, was completed in 1990 and has formed a reservoir of 315 square miles (815 sq km). In order to keep this reservoir full, Turkey creates regular interruptions in the flow of the Euphrates; this affects the amount of water that flows into Syria and Iraq. Some estimates indicate that when the Southeast Anatolia Project is completed, it will reduce the flow from the Euphrates by about 40 percent to Syria and 90 percent to Iraq.

Syrian projects also reduce the amount of water from the Euphrates that reaches Iraq. The Al Thawrah Dam, built by Syria during the 1970s, created the Assad Reservoir. This significantly diminished the flow of water reaching Iraq.

If the level of the Euphrates River falls too low, water shortages in Iraq can result. Water from the Tharthar Reservoir, which is fed by the Tigris River, can be diverted into the Euphrates when it is low. In the past, however, the reservoir has not held an adequate supply to overcome the lack of water resulting from Syrian and Turkish projects. As a consequence, the relationship between the three nations has been strained at times. In 1998 Syria and Iraq agreed to work together to oppose the Southeast Anatolia Project, but their attempts to halt the project have been unsuccessful.

THE REGIONS

Geographically, the country of Iraq can be divided into four distinct regions. One is the southern *alluvial* plain, which begins just northwest of Baghdad and stretches southeast to the Persian Gulf.

A second region is the desert plateau, which is located in western and southwestern Iraq on the borders of Syria, Jordan, and Saudi Arabia. The third region is the Jazirah (from the Arabic word for "island"). The Jazirah is a wedge-shaped territory in the northwest that touches Syria; it is bounded on the west by the Euphrates and on the east by the Tigris. A final region, the northeastern highlands, includes the Zagros Mountains, which are located along the border with Iran.

Vivian Block, who once taught English in the southern city of Basra, vividly remembers her impressions of the alluvial plain as she traveled by train north to Baghdad. "Looking out the window,

Quick Facts: The Geography of Iraq

Location: Middle East, bordering the Persian Gulf, between Iran and Kuwait
Area: (slightly more than twice the size of Idaho)
    total: 168,754 square miles (437,072 sq km)
    land: 166,858 square miles (432,162 sq km)
    water: 1,896 square miles (4,910 sq km)
Borders: Iran, 906 miles (1,458 km); Jordan, 113 miles (181 km); Kuwait, 149 miles (240 km); Saudi Arabia, 506 miles (814 km); Syria, 376 miles (605 km); Turkey, 219 miles (352 km)
Climate: mostly desert; mild to cool winters with dry, hot, cloudless summers; northern mountainous regions along Iranian and Turkish borders experience cold winters with occasionally heavy snows that melt in early spring, sometimes causing extensive flooding in central and southern Iraq
Terrain: mostly broad plains; reedy marshes along Iranian border in south with large flooded areas; mountains along borders with Iran and Turkey
Elevation extremes:
    lowest point: Persian Gulf, 0 feet
    highest point: Mt. Ebrahim, 11,811 feet (3,600 meters)
Natural hazards: dust storms, sandstorms, floods

Source: CIA World Factbook, 2015.

we saw flat, arid ground. . . . The landscape, which was mostly desert, would have patches of green that a gardener attended to with daily irrigation. [I could see] alfalfa, onions, grasses, a celery-tasting herb called crufus, and parsley, as well as palm trees bearing dates."

The alluvial plain makes up about one-third of Iraq. The entire plain is flat with a low elevation, dropping from 80 feet above sea

Located along the Iraq-Iran border, the Shatt al Arab has been a source of frequent conflict between the two countries.

level near the city of Ramadi on the Euphrates to sea level in the south along the Persian Gulf.

Two large lakes dominate the landscape. One, Lake As-Saniyah, is just west of the Tigris and runs southwest from the town of Ali al-Gharbi for 75 miles (121 km). The second and more swampy lake, Al-Hammar, is farther south and extends from Basra to Suq ash-Shuyukh.

The Shatt al Arab is located in the south of the alluvial plain. Two of its tributaries are the Karkheh and the Karun Rivers, which flow into the Shatt from Iran just above Iraq's delta on the Persian Gulf. As a result of these rivers, the area near the Gulf is filled with small lakes and marshes that spread over the landscape. The delta continues to grow as silt collects from the rivers. Continual dredging is necessary in order to keep the Shatt al Arab open for navigation to Basra.

A second distinct region is the desert plateau, located in western and southwestern Iraq. This barren area makes up about one-third of the country. It is the least-developed part of Iraq, and few people live in the desert, which is an extension of the Syrian and Arabian deserts. The flatness of the land is broken by a number of **wadis** running east and west, some for hundreds of miles. The few remaining Bedouins of Iraq live in this vast, dry area.

The western desert near Jordan rises to 100 feet (31 meters) and is called the Wadiyah. In the southern part of the desert plateau is a sandy, gravelly plain called Al-Diddibah, which borders the western part of Kuwait. Its elevation ascends from about 300 feet (93 meters) near Kuwait to 3,000 feet (915 meters) where Saudi Arabia and Jordan intersect with Iraq to the west.

On the northern edge of the desert plateau is a highway that runs from Baghdad to Amman, the capital of Jordan, and to Damascus, the capital of Syria. Along this highway is the busy trading center of Rutbah, one of the very few towns on the plateau.

The Jazirah region is located in the northwest, along the border with Syria. It is a desert plateau that descends from an average of 1,475 feet (450 meters) above sea level near Syria to about 260 feet (79 meters) above sea level just north of Baghdad. Most of the population of this region is located along the Tigris and Euphrates Rivers and in a small area of the north where rain allows agriculture. In the rest of the region the population is sparse and development is limited.

The rain-fed agricultural section of the Jazirah is near the Syrian border. There, wheat and barley can be grown without the necessity of irrigation. This area, which has been cultivated for thousands of years, was once known as the granary of the ancient world.

Mosul, Iraq's second-largest city, is the largest settlement within the Jazirah and the main center of activity for the northern third of the country. Mosul Province is the location of almost 80 percent of Iraq's vast oil reserves. At one time cotton was the main export of the province, and the word *muslin* (a type of cotton fabric) was derived from the city's name.

The fourth region of Iraq is called the northeastern highlands; it is part of a larger area known as Kurdistan, where most of Iraq's Kurdish population lives. The highlands contain rugged, almost inaccessible mountains. The elevation of this area ascends from 655 feet (200 meters) at the Tigris River to nearly 6,000 feet (1,830 meters) on the ridge tops. From there the mountain peaks soar to more than 11,000 feet (3,355 meters). The highest elevation in Iraq is Mount Ebrahim, which rises to a height of 11,811 feet (3,600 meters). At the higher elevations, the mountain peaks are covered with snow for half of the year. The Zagros Mountains are rugged, with only a few passes through them. The Rawanduze River Gorge, which connects Iraq and Iran, is the best known of these mountain passes.

The mountains contain Iraq's only forests. The steeper slopes

The Zagros Mountains are a mountainous area of Kurdistan, in northern Iraq near the border with Iran and Turkey.

permit only grazing for cattle, sheep, and goats, but on the lower, gentler slopes people cultivate fruit and nut trees.

Several streams in the highlands flow southeast into the Tigris, including the Khabur, Great Zab, Little Zab, Udhaym, and Diyala. The Iraqi government began hydraulic projects along some of these rivers in the 1950s. The Kukan Dam and reservoir and the Debs Dam were built on the Little Zab, and the Darbandikhan Dam and reservoir were constructed on the upper Diyala.

FLORA AND FAUNA

There is little vegetation in most of Iraq. In the Zagros Mountains, forests of oak, maple, and hawthorn trees still exist, although in recent years the size of these forests has been reduced because of overcutting. The rest of the country contains few trees, except for the date palm and the poplar, which grow along the rivers.

Although millennia of human habitation have reduced the amount of wildlife living in Iraq, many animals still make this land their home. Mammals that can be seen in Iraq include cheetahs, gazelles, antelopes, wild asses, hyenas, wolves, jackals, wild pigs, and rabbits. Many birds of prey, such as vultures, buzzards, ravens, and hawks, continue to soar above the landscape. Other birds common to Iraq include ducks, geese, and partridges. Closer to the ground, numerous types of reptiles and lizards can be found. There are many domesticated animals, such as camels, oxen, water buffalo, and horses, and flocks of sheep and goats can be found on mountainsides.

THE CLIMATE AND THE WINDS

The climate of Iraq is fairly similar throughout the country, with the exception of the north. Mosul's January temperature averages 44° Fahrenheit (6° Celsius); in July, the average temperature in Mosul is about 90°F (32°C). Winter and summer temperatures are much lower in the high elevations of the Zagros Mountains. Baghdad's average temperature is about 50°F (10°C) in January and about 95°F (35°C) in July. Temperatures in the southern alluvial plain, however, can reach 123°F (51°C) in the summer.

There are two wind patterns in the country. The eastern wind, called *sharki*, is hot, dry, and dusty; it can gust at up to 50 miles per hour (81 km per hour) and create massive dust storms. The *sharki* winds can occur throughout the year, although they are more frequent during the summer months. The other wind is known as *shammal*; it is a steady, gentle wind that comes from the north and brings great relief during the extreme heat of the summer months.

The northeastern highlands receive ample rainfall from October to May, so the lower levels of this region are suitable for farming and are home to a large population. By contrast, the southeastern alluvial plain receives only about 6 inches (15 centimeters) of rain each year. As a result, agriculture there depends entirely upon irrigation. There is almost no rainfall at all in the western and southwestern desert plateau, which covers about one-third of Iraq.

 Text-Dependent Questions

1. What is the ancient name for the land between the Tigris and Euphrates Rivers?
2. Where is the Jazirah region? What is this area of Iraq like?
3. What is the best-known pass through the Zagros Mountains?

 Research Project

Using the Internet or your school library, find out about the sort of creatures that live in the deserts of Iraq. Choose one, and write a short report about it. Tell what the animal looks like, whether it is dangerous, what it eats, and how it survives in the harsh climate. Find photos online to include with your report, and present it to the class.

Mesopotamia produced the world's earliest known civilization, Sumer, as well as the oldest known system of writing, cuneiform. The clay tablet shown here, which is covered with cuneiform writing, is important for another reason: it is the prologue to the Code of Hammurabi, one of the earliest legal codes, which dates to the 18th century BCE.

Iraq's History to 1990

In 1901 a group of French archaeologists traveled to Mesopotamia to search for the remains of an ancient civilization. As the archaeologists dug into the sun-baked earth, they hit a large object. Digging carefully, they uncovered an eight-foot-long block of black basalt. Across the face of the huge stone were words carved in a language unfamiliar to the archaeologists. It was evidence of the powerful kingdom they had sought.

When the writings on the basalt slab were translated, they were found to be the laws of Hammurabi, a great ruler of Babylon who had lived around 1750 BCE. The Code of Hammurabi, as the laws are called, is one of the earliest written legal systems; it gives modern students valuable insight into the structure of ancient Mesopotamian society.

By the time of Hammurabi, civilization in Mesopotamia had already existed for some two and a half millennia. Mesopotamia is often called the "cradle of civilization" because archaeologists believe that it is the place where human settlements first evolved into a society with complex social and political organization and advanced cultural achievements. **Nomadic** hunter-gatherers may have settled in the area between the Tigris and Euphrates Rivers as early as 9000 BCE. They used the river water for agriculture and began to domesticate animals such as sheep and dogs. As these hunters tied themselves to the land and depended on farming for their food, they began to build villages. Over thousands of years, these would evolve into city-states and, eventually, kingdoms and empires.

Sumer, considered the world's first civilization, was the most famous of the early Mesopotamian empires. By the 24th century BCE, the Sumerian cities had been unified into an empire. The Sumerians are credited with many inventions. One of these was cuneiform writing, in which long reeds were used to make wedge-shaped characters on tablets of soft clay; these tablets were later baked to make them hard, preserving the writing. Hundreds of thousands of cuneiform tablets have been found and translated,

Words to Understand in This Chapter

coup—the sudden, and often violent, overthrow of a government by a small group.

mandate—an order given by the League of Nations to one of its members for that member to help establish a responsible government in a former colony.

nomadic—having no fixed home but moving from place to place.

regent—someone who governs a kingdom when the king is under age or is away.

secular—not religious; concerned with the present world.

shah—a Persian king or ruler.

sheikh—a term of respect and authority given to an Arab tribal leader, or to the ruler of a small kingdom called a sheikhdom.

giving insights into daily life in Mesopotamia. Sumerians also developed such important tools as the wheel and the plow, and they created a form of banking.

As the centuries passed, empires rose and fell in Mesopotamia. One of the greatest of the later ones was Assyria, the largest empire the ancient world had ever seen. The empire lasted from about 1400 to 612 BCE. At the height of their influence the Assyrians controlled land from the Mediterranean Sea to the Caspian Sea, and from the Persian Gulf to the Red Sea. The ruins of Nineveh, the capital of Assyria, are located near the city of Mosul, Iraq.

In 612 BCE Nineveh was destroyed by another growing Mesopotamian power, the Babylonians. One of the most influential Babylonian rulers was King Nebuchadnezzar, who built Babylon into the most beautiful city in the ancient world. He created the famous "hanging gardens," with trees, plants, and flowers growing on a tiered structure held by arches 400 feet (122 meters) above the ground. The Hanging Gardens of Babylon were proclaimed one of the Seven Wonders of the Ancient World.

The remains of Nebuchadnezzar's palace in Babylon. Nebuchadnezzar, a seventh-century BCE king of Babylon, built the Hanging Gardens of Babylon, one of the Seven Wonders of the Ancient World.

However, Nebuchadnezzar's descendants did not remain in power for long. Babylon fell to the Medes and Persians (people from the modern-day state of Iran) in 539 BCE. Under Cyrus the Great, the Persian Achaemenid Empire was established; the Achaemenids ruled Mesopotamia and most of the Middle East for the next 250 years. During this time the communities of Mesopotamia fell into decline, and Babylon and other cities withered and decayed.

In the fourth century BCE, the Achaemenids were defeated by the armies of the Macedonian conqueror Alexander the Great. Alexander's conquests brought Hellenistic culture to the region, and he planned to rebuild Babylon and make it an administrative center of his vast empire. However, Alexander died in Babylon in 323 BCE, before these plans could be carried out. Alexander's Greek generals remained in power in Mesopotamia until 126 BCE, when the Parthians, a people from northern Persia, took control of the region.

The Parthian rulers who controlled Mesopotamia were often in conflict with the Roman Empire, which controlled the lands adjacent to the Mediterranean Sea (such as Syria). Roman legions occupied Mesopotamia for brief periods—from CE 98 to 117 and from 193 to 211. After 227, a new group came to power in Persia: the Sassanids. They soon took control of Mesopotamia as well.

After the Roman Empire split during the fourth century, the Sassanids continued fighting with the Eastern Roman, or Byzantine, Empire. From the city of Constantinople, in modern-day Turkey, the Christian Byzantines dominated the eastern Mediterranean and North Africa. The Sassanids and the Byzantines struggled with one another for centuries, competing for territories and trade routes. But by the seventh century, the world of the Middle East underwent a radical change with the rise of a new religion, Islam.

THE RISE OF ISLAM

Around 570, Muhammad ibn Abdullah was born on the Arabian

Peninsula. For many years the communities of Arabia had been prosperous because of trade. Muhammad lived in the city of Mecca; when he grew up he married a wealthy widow and became a successful merchant.

At the time, the people of the Arabian Peninsula were pagans who worshiped many gods. One god, Allah, was believed to have created the earth, but in general Allah was given no more or less attention than any of the other Arab gods. According to tradition, however, Muhammad grew up worshipping only Allah.

When he was about 40 years old, Muhammad received a series of divine messages, which said that Allah was the only true God. Muhammad was told to spread this message to the people of Arabia. He began to call on his neighbors in Mecca to give up their other, false gods and surrender their lives to Allah. (The word *Islam* comes from an Arabic word meaning "submission" or "surrender.")

At first, the people of Mecca tolerated the teachings of Muhammad, though he attracted few followers. Eventually, however, Mecca's pagan leaders decided to do away with the annoying preacher. They plotted to kill Muhammad, but he got wind of the plot. In 622 Muhammad and his followers fled Mecca, journeying to another city, Medina, which was several hundred miles to the north.

The people of Medina welcomed Muhammad and listened to his message. The ranks of Muslims—as followers of Islam are called—grew rapidly.

Two years after the flight to Medina, Muhammad's followers and a force of Meccans fought a major battle at the village of Badr. The Muslims won decisively, but in the ensuing years the two sides fought many skirmishes and an occasional pitched battle. Finally, in 629, Muhammad returned to Mecca with a small army. The people of Mecca surrendered without bloodshed, and many converted to Islam.

Muhammad's disciples wrote down and organized his teachings

into a book, the Qur'an (or Koran). Devout Muslims consider the Qur'an to be the direct word of God, and therefore a holy, perfect scripture.

After the capitulation of Mecca, Muhammad sent envoys throughout the Arab world, inviting the scattered tribes to become Muslims. Most of the tribes quickly joined; those that did not were conquered by the growing Muslim armies and forced to convert at the point of a sword. By the time of Muhammad's death in 632, Islam had spread throughout the Arabian Peninsula and north into Syria.

Islam came to the region of modern-day Iraq shortly after Muhammad's death. In 634 the Islamic caliph, who was selected to lead the Muslims after Muhammad, sent his armies on raids into Mesopotamia. In a series of battles between 634 and 636, the Arabs soundly defeated the Sassanid forces, despite being outnumbered six to one.

At this time, most people living in Mesopotamia followed Christianity. The Muslims allowed them to practice their religion, so long as they paid a special tax to the conquering Arabs. Arab settlers also poured into Mesopotamia from Arabia, living along the fertile plains of the Tigris and Euphrates. Over time, the natives of Mesopotamia intermarried with the Arab newcomers, and most converted to Islam.

The Iraq area was the site of a major division in the Islamic faith—the break between Sunni and Shiite Muslims. The split arose out of a disagreement over who should be the caliph. Most Muslims supported the selection of the caliph based on his piety; these became known as the Sunni Muslims. However, a minority insisted that the caliph should be a member of Muhammad's family—particularly, the prophet's son-in-law Ali and his descendants. These Muslims became known as Shiites. The Shiites also felt that the Sunni caliphs misinterpreted the Qur'an. The two groups fought for power until the Battle of Karbala in 680, when the Shiite leader

Hussein was slain along with his family and 200 of his followers. Iraqi cities such as An Najaf and Karbala remain important shrines for Shiite Muslims today. After the defeat of the Shiites, the Sunni caliphs maintained their control over Islam.

For the next seven centuries, two Sunni dynasties ruled the Muslims—the Umayyads from 661 to 750 and the Abbasids from 750 to 1258. The caliphs ruled the spreading Islamic empire first from Medina, and then from Damascus, Syria. In 762 the administrative center was moved to a new city on the Tigris River, called Madinat as-Salam ("the City of Peace"), although many people still knew it by the name of a small town that had been on that site before—Baghdad.

During the eighth century, Muslim culture blossomed in Baghdad. Literature, science, art, and mathematics flourished, and Baghdad became one of the world's leading cities. The caliphs encouraged the growth of knowledge by opening schools that attracted scholars from all over. The writings of ancient Greece and Rome were translated into Arabic and preserved in libraries and universities in Baghdad and other cities. Many of these important writings had been lost in the West when barbarians destroyed the Roman Empire; they would be rediscovered by European scholars centuries later. The 8th through the 12th centuries are often considered to be the golden age of the Arab Islamic civilization.

The area of modern-day Iraq continued to be at the center of the Islamic civilization until the 13th century. During the early years of that century, the Mongols had spread their control east from Asia into Persia under the great leader Genghis Khan. In 1258 Mongol armies sacked Baghdad. The city was destroyed, and most of the inhabitants were slaughtered—in fact, the Mongol leader Hülegü Khan, grandson of Genghis Khan, made a pyramid from the skulls of poets, scholars, and religious leaders in Baghdad. During the next few centuries, control of Mesopotamia alternated between the Mongols and local rulers; in general, however, the region fell into decline.

CONFLICT OVER THE REGION

By the 15th century, a new power was rising in the Middle East—the Ottoman Turks. In 1453 the Ottomans conquered Constantinople, ending the 1,000-year history of the Byzantine Empire. The Ottoman Turks were Sunni Muslims who were dedicated to the faith, but they also wanted to expand their own power throughout the region. By the early 16th century, the Ottomans were extending their empire into Syria, Egypt, and Arabia, and they turned their sights on Mesopotamia to the south.

During the same period, the Safavid Empire had come to power in Persia to the east. The Safavid rulers declared Shia Islam to be the official religion of Persia, and they wanted to control Iraq in part because it contained the important Shiite shrines at An Najaf and Karbala. Fighting between the Ottomans and Safavids continued for more than a century. The Safavid armies conquered Mesopotamia in 1509, but the Ottomans took control of the region in 1535. The Safavids retook Baghdad in 1623, but lost the city to the Ottomans in 1638.

The Ottoman Empire would maintain control over Mesopotamia until the early years of the 20th century. An Ottoman governor was placed in Baghdad, and important families were given positions in the Ottoman government. The Ottomans divided Mesopotamia into three provinces—a northern province governed from Mosul, a central province ruled from Baghdad, and a southern province controlled from Basra. Outside of these cities, however, the power of the Ottoman officials was limited. Instead, local tribal chiefs called **sheikhs** had the real authority in rural Mesopotamia. Although they paid taxes to the Ottomans, these sheikhs had a great deal of independence.

The Mongols' sack of Baghdad in 1258 was considerably more violent than this illustration from a Persian manuscript might indicate. The conquerors laid waste to the magnificent city and slaughtered most of its inhabitants. The Mongol leader, Hülegü Khan, even constructed a pyramid from the skulls of the dead.

By the end of the 19th century, widespread unrest had developed in Mesopotamia. This occurred in part because of a land law that had been passed by the Ottoman government in 1858. Before passage of this law, the Arabs did not recognize private ownership of land. Those who used the land and could hold it occupied the land. But under the land law, the Ottoman government allowed people to register their claim to land, and the government would recognize them as the owners of the property.

The land law affected the way power was distributed in the region. Traditionally, Arab sheikhs had ruled with the consent of

The Ottoman Turks capture Constantinople, 1453. During the following century, the Ottoman Empire extended its control into Kurdistan and Mesopotamia, in present-day Iraq. Ottoman influence in the region would last until the second decade of the 20th century.

others in the tribe, and they were supposed to make decisions based on what was best for the tribe. But after the rural sheikhs and the important families in Baghdad registered their claims to land, they were obliged to support the Ottoman government, which could back up their land claims with military force. Most of the ordinary tribesmen became little more than tenant farmers, with their labor enriching the landowning families.

During the 19th century, contact with the nations of Europe

began to increase. The opening of the Suez Canal by France in 1869, and the strong presence of Great Britain, which had treaties with a number of small Arab kingdoms on the Gulf, brought the people of Mesopotamia into contact with Western ideas and technology.

Meanwhile, at the very heart of the Ottoman Empire in Istanbul, a new ideology, nationalism, was beginning to supplant the old religion-based legitimacy of the empire. Nationalist Turks wished to create a **secular** Turkish state, in which all of the people would share a common ethnic background, culture, or heritage. In 1908 a group of young Turkish officers (who became known in the West as the "Young Turks") mounted a resistance movement against Sultan Abdul Hamid II. Taking control of parliament, they staged an election for a new parliament representative of Turkey. Rule by the Young Turks was followed by the Committee of Union and Progress (CUP), which controlled the remnants of the Ottoman Empire until 1918. This period of Turkish nationalism resulted in political and cultural repression of Arabs in the Ottoman Empire. Use of the Arabic language was banned, and leaders who supported the idea of Arab nationalism were arrested.

Everything would change after the start of the First World War in 1914. The Ottoman Empire entered the war on the side of the Central Powers, Germany and Austria-Hungary. Great Britain, fighting on the side of the Allies, landed troops near Basra in November 1914 to seize this Ottoman territory on the Gulf. By March 1917, British troops had captured Baghdad; by the time the war ended, the British controlled the region as far north as Mosul. Great Britain also encouraged the Arabs to rise up against their Ottoman rulers. Under the leadership of Hussein bin Ali, the sharif of Mecca, some Arabs launched a revolt in 1916. At the war's conclusion in 1918, Arab forces controlled much of present-day Jordan, Syria, and the Arabian Peninsula.

THE BRITISH MANDATE

After the end of the First World War, an armistice line was drawn north of Mosul, leaving the British firmly in control of all three of the former Ottoman provinces in Mesopotamia.

The British and their allies had encouraged the Great Arab Revolt by making vague promises to Arab nationalists that the region would be united as an Arab state. However, when the war ended, a newly created international organization, the League of Nations, divided the Arab region into a number of smaller territories. At the 1919 Paris Peace Conference, Great Britain was given a ***mandate*** to rule Mesopotamia, as well as other territories in the Middle East. The area of the British Mesopotamian mandate was also given a new name, Iraq, from an Arabic word meaning "shoreline." This term had previously been used to designate the southern part of the country.

Some of the Arab leaders felt the British mandate was just a way to bring their country into the British Empire. They had a legitimate reason to worry, because British officials were discussing whether England should directly rule the territory or help it develop self-government. Under the League of Nations' mandate system, the established European governments were supposed to help the former Ottoman territories build governments and rule themselves. But the European powers seemed to be interested in making the mandate areas part of their colonial empires. France, for example, had been given the League of Nations mandate to rule Syria and Lebanon in April 1920. The month before, a Syrian national congress had selected a king for Syria—Faisal, the son of Sharif Hussein bin Ali. After the French arrived, they forced Faisal to flee the country, then set up their own government.

There were other problems with the mandate that created Iraq. For one, the population of the region was quite disparate. For example, more than 50 percent of the people of Iraq were Arab Shiite Muslims, about 20 percent were Arab Sunni Muslims, and about 20 percent were Kurdish Sunni Muslims. There were also Kurdish Shiites and Arab Christians living in the country. In addition to the historic differences between the Sunni and Shiite Muslims, there are important ethnic and cultural differences between Arabs and Kurds, who have their own language and traditions. However, under the centuries of Ottoman rule, the minority Sunni Arabs had gained a great amount of land and power; the Shiites had been sub-

The decisions of the so-called Big Four leaders (from left: Prime Minister David Lloyd George of Great Britain, Prime Minister Vittorio Orlando of Italy, Prime Minister Georges Clemenceau of France, and President Woodrow Wilson of the United States) during the Paris Peace Conference of 1919 shaped the world—often in unforeseen ways—for decades to come. It was at Paris that the nation of Iraq was created.

ject to Ottoman discrimination. Most of the government officials in Baghdad and officers in the army were Arab Sunni Muslims, and they were determined to maintain their control over the region by resisting the British.

By mid-1920, central Iraq was in the hands of the Sunni Arabs; however, by the end of October 1920 the British had brought the revolt under control. But when Britain created a new government for Iraq, most of the government officials and the officers of the new Iraqi army were members of the Sunni Arab families that had held power under the Ottoman Turks. The British, though, chose the king of Iraq—36-year-old Prince Faisal, who assumed the throne on August 23, 1921.

King Faisal did not have much support from the leading families and tribes of Iraq, who saw the king as a foreigner (he was a member of thc Hashemite family of the western Arabian Peninsula) and a puppet of the Western powers. Faisal's goal was to develop Iraq

Though he had never even visited Iraq, Faisal I, a member of the Hashemite family, was the British choice as Iraq's king.

into a unified country with loyalty to a central government, but the many diverse groups in Iraq and the political power of the Sunni Muslim minority would limit success.

The Kurdish people of northern Iraq also opposed the monarchy. The 1920 treaty that established Iraq and other countries initially called for a Kurdish state in the mountainous region known as Kurdistan, which included parts of Iraq, Turkey, Iran, Armenia, and Syria. However, the new governments of these areas decided against establishing a Kurdish state. In Iraq, it was determined that the Kurds should have some control over the government of their northern province. For the Kurds, however, this was not enough: they revolted against the British-supported monarchy from 1922 to 1924 and again in 1932. Both times their attempts to separate were crushed.

As the capital of the monarchy, Baghdad became the center of power. Land became the reward for those who found favor with the king. Iraqis who gained influential government positions used their authority to reward family members or friends. And the monarchy remained subordinate to Great Britain, which exercised extensive control over Iraq's internal affairs as well as its foreign relations.

OIL AND THE MONARCHY

During the 1920s, oil became an important element in the development of Iraq. Before World War I, the Ottoman Turks had agreed to allow the Turkish Petroleum Company—a group of British, Dutch, French, and American investors—to search for oil in Mesopotamia. After the Iraqi monarchy was formed, the Western powers pressured King Faisal to give up Iraq's right to the country's oil in exchange for annual royalty payments.

In 1927 oil was discovered in northeast Iraq near Kirkuk. The Iraqi government agreed to give the oil company (renamed the Iraq Petroleum Company) exclusive rights to explore for oil in all of northeastern Iraq. By 1931 oil revenues made up 20 percent of government income, and oil had begun to be a source of power to those in office.

During this time, however, Arab nationalists continued to oppose both the British presence in Iraq and the monarchy of King Faisal. In 1929 Great Britain announced its plan to end its mandate over Iraq and allow the country to become independent. In October 1932 Iraq joined the League of Nations as an independent nation. However, British influence over the king remained strong, and a treaty between Britain and Iraq permitted British forces to use air bases in the country.

Continuing tensions between Arabs and Kurds, as well as among Sunnis, Shiites, and Christians, prevented the government from achieving stability. There were also problems with the region's borders, which had been drawn arbitrarily by the European powers. The boundaries limited trade outside of the country, contributing to an economic depression, and also led to skirmishes between Iraq and its neighbors Saudi Arabia, Iran, Turkey, and Syria.

When King Faisal died suddenly in 1933, the crown went to his 21-year-old son, Ghazi. However, the new king was unable to manage the factions within Iraq's government. During the years of his rule, many problems surfaced or got worse. Tribes in the remote areas of Iraq revolted against the central government, and in the north the Kurds tried to gain independence. At the same time, Iran reopened an old dispute with Iraq over the use of the Shatt al Arab waterway, part of the border between their two countries. To gain more control of the waterway, Iran challenged the border.

At the height of the tensions, in 1939, King Ghazi was killed in a car crash. His son, Faisal II, became king, but because the boy was only three years old, his uncle, Abdulillah, became **regent**, with authority to rule until Faisal II was old enough to take the throne.

In September 1939 the Second World War began in Europe when

the armies of Nazi Germany invaded Poland. As the German war machine rolled over Europe, crushing France by June 1940, Great Britain found itself in a desperate struggle against the Nazis. Because many Arab nationalists in Iraq did not like British influence over their government, some officers in the Iraqi army supported the German dictator Adolf Hitler. In 1941 these officers revolted against the administration of Abdulillah, forcing the regent to flee the country.

To restore order, British troops landed in Iraq, put down the **coup**, and placed Abdulillah back in charge of the government. When he was returned to power, Abdulillah tried to purge Iraq of those who dissented with his rule, imprisoning or executing many nationalists and establishing tight restrictions.

After World War II ended in 1945, Iraqi society grew more open. The press, which had been censored during the war, was allowed greater freedom. Political parties, once banned, were given permission to organize. When the economy weakened, though, unrest grew. The government again began to limit freedom, increasing dissatisfaction with the monarchy. Other events in the Middle East would also lead to unrest, particularly the conflict in the area of British Palestine.

After the First World War, the region along the eastern Mediterranean coast known as Palestine had been placed under British rule by the League of Nations. In ancient times the region had been the homeland of the Jewish people; some Jews had never left the land, while others arrived as settlers during the 19th and early 20th centuries. At the same time, Arabs who had lived in the land for centuries were not happy about the arrival of these Jewish settlers, and they often attacked settlements. During World War II, the Nazis had attempted to carry out Hitler's "final solution"—the extermination of the Jews—and approximately 6 million European Jews were killed in concentration camps. After the end of the war, many survivors of the Holocaust left Europe for Palestine, where they hoped to build a Jewish state. Violence between Jews and Arabs began to escalate.

In 1947 the United Nations, an international organization that replaced the failed League of Nations, proposed dividing Palestine into Arab and Jewish states, with Jerusalem, a city regarded as holy by Jews, Muslims, and Christians, to be open to everyone under the auspices of the U.N. Great Britain, which still ruled the area under its League of Nations mandate, did not agree with this decision and announced its intention to withdraw from Palestine in May 1948. The Palestinian Arabs also voiced their opposition to the U.N. partition plan, and with other Arab countries they made plans to destroy the Jewish settlers once the British pulled out.

Israel declared its independence on May 15, 1948, the day after the British left Palestine. The United States and the U.S.S.R. quickly recognized Israel as an independent state. But Arab armies from Egypt, Jordan, Syria, and Iraq immediately attacked Israel. Iraq provided the largest force—some 15,000 well-trained soldiers. The Arabs expected a quick victory. However, to their surprise—and to the surprise of the world—the determined Israelis outfought the Arabs and expanded their territory before a cease-fire ended the conflict in early 1949.

The new Jewish state soon had a large influx of immigrants. Jewish communities had existed in Arab lands for hundreds of years, but many Jews—aware now of a growing hostility toward them in the Arab world—chose to move to Israel. In 1947 an estimated 117,000 Jews had lived in Iraq; many of their ancestors had been brought to Babylon as captives after the conquest of Jerusalem around 597 BCE. By 1952 Jews living in Iraq numbered fewer than 5,000.

The 1950s also saw oil become an even more important part of Iraq's economy. By 1952 most of the money brought into Iraq came from the production of oil. As a result, huge amounts of money were now available to those who controlled the government.

During the 1940s and 1950s, Nuri al-Said was an important political figure in Iraq. His views favored the countries of the West—in particular, Great Britain and the United States. He held the office of prime minister several times—but even when he was not in public office, Said wielded great power in the country. With his pro-Western position, he angered many Iraqis who still resented the British presence in Iraq's affairs. Said was not interested in democracy, however, and built his own power on personal relationships and ties with important families within Iraq. He formed a political party, Hizb al-Ittihad Al Dusturi (the Constitutional Union Party), and used it for his own advancement.

After the Constitutional Union Party won a majority in the 1953 elections, Nuri became Iraq's minister of defense. One of his goals was to make the army completely obedient to the state, because he realized that an independent army corps could be dangerous to his ambitions. Although most of the senior officers supported Nuri, many younger officers did not. They secretly formed a group called the Free Officers and began to talk about resistance to the government.

The concept of Arab nationalism—of building a single state in which the Arabs were united—had never gone away. The problem with this concept was that nearly every Arab leader thought he should be the head of the united Arab state. But during this time the strongest of the Arab leaders was Gamal Abdel Nasser, who had come to power in Egypt in 1952. Nasser wanted to bring about a pan-Arab state, headed by Egypt, the largest Arab country. He also wanted to modernize Egypt and undertook a series of development projects. In 1956, after British and U.S. financial assistance dried up following Egypt's purchase of Soviet arms, Nasser announced that he would nationalize the Suez Canal. This decision sparked a joint attack, for the purposes of securing the canal, by France,

Britain, and Israel. But the actions of these American allies—at the height of the Cold War—worried U.S. leaders, who feared that permitting the seizure of the canal would drive the Arab states to the side of the communist U.S.S.R. The United States used its influence to force the British, French, and Israelis to withdraw.

Though the Egyptian army had been defeated on the battlefield, Nasser became a hero in the Arab world. His defiance of the West inspired the Arab nationalists. In Iraq, the Free Officers admired Nasser and wanted their own country to follow the same independent, anti-Western course. Demonstrations against the monarchy were held in the major cities of Iraq throughout 1956.

YEARS OF REVOLUTION AND UNREST

More Iraqi military officers joined the Free Officers after the 1956 Suez crisis. By 1958 the Free Officers had agreed that they would overthrow the monarchy. They secretly formed a Supreme Committee, with one of their officers, General Abd al-Karim Qasim, as chairman.

Although King Faisal II had come of age in May 1953, the regent Abdulillah continued to exercise great influence in the government, as did Nuri al-Said.

In 1958 two of the largest Arab states, Egypt and Syria, announced they would form a political organization, the United Arab Republic. This merger would increase their influence over their neighbors. In response, the Hashemite rulers of Jordan and Iraq formed their own organization, the Arab Union, in February 1958.

When unrest developed in Lebanon during July 1958, Nuri al-Said decided to send Iraqi troops into Jordan to support the pro-West Hashemite government there. On July 13, Iraqi troops stationed in eastern Iraq were ordered to Jordan. On the way, as the army passed through Baghdad, General Abd al-Karim Qasim ordered the soldiers to seize all important buildings in Baghdad, including the radio station. When they controlled the radio and government buildings, the Free Officers announced that they had overthrown the monarchy and were forming a republic. Nuri al-Said, King Faisal II, Abdulillah, and other government leaders and members of the royal family were taken from their homes and executed.

Qasim became prime minister, minister of defense, and commander-in-chief of the military, while another officer, Colonel Abd al-Salam Arif, took over other important leadership positions. It wasn't long, however, before the two disagreed on the direction the new government should take. Arif wanted the Arab people to be united in a single country, and he was willing to join with Egypt's Nasser to make that happen. Qasim, on the other hand, wanted to see Iraq become a strong Arab power, and he did not want to be subordinate to Nasser.

Qasim repressed all opposition, and soon he imprisoned Arif and

Prince Abdulillah, the Iraqi regent, hands over power to Faisal II in a ceremony on the latter's 18th birthday, May 2, 1953. Despite the end of his official role, Abdulillah continued to exert considerable influence on the new Iraqi king.

other Free Officers who disagreed with him. He maintained control in the same way that Iraqi leaders had under the monarchy—rewarding those who supported him and dealing harshly with those who did not. Street demonstrations became common as different groups struggled for power, both within the civilian government and the military.

Political parties began to develop increased influence in Iraqi politics. Since the Iraqi Communist Party was the only long-established political party in Iraq, Qasim looked to it for support. It was composed mostly of the thwarted and powerless, the Shia and Kurds. Another group, the Baath (Renaissance) Party, had been active in Iraq for several years; the Baath Party was a small, secretive group of Arab nationalists. The original Baath Party had formed in Syria in the 1940s, and a branch of the party had emerged in Iraq during 1951. The party appealed to some young people in Iraq because Baath leaders criticized the power of the landowners and emphasized the need for pan-Arabism.

The Arab nationalists created an uprising against the Communists in Mosul in March 1959. Qasim stamped out the revolt with a sweeping massacre. Another demonstration occurred in the city of Kirkuk on July 14, 1959, the anniversary of the overthrow of the monarchy. Qasim again ruthlessly suppressed the dissenters and arrested many Arab nationalists leaders.

As Qasim grew more and more unpopular in Mosul and Kirkuk, the leaders of the Baath Party decided they could attract new followers by assassinating him. Their attempt in October of 1959 was unsuccessful, although the Baath conspirators killed a guard and wounded Qasim. One of the assassins was a 22-year-old named Saddam Hussein, who escaped arrest by fleeing to Cairo, Egypt.

In June 1961, the nearby country of Kuwait declared its independence after years of British rule. Qasim publicly claimed that Kuwait rightfully belonged to Iraq and that he wanted it to be annexed to his country. He argued that the League of Nations should have included that territory in the nation of Iraq in 1923, since it had been part of the Basra province under the Ottoman Empire. Qasim further argued that the British had deliberately separated it from Iraq to block Iraq's access to the Persian Gulf.

The British, fearing that Qasim would seize Iraq's defenseless neighbor, sent troops to Kuwait. The Arab League, to show its opposition to Qasim's claims, admitted Kuwait as a member. By the end of the summer, troops from the Arab League replaced the British soldiers. As a result, Iraq broke off diplomatic relations with many Arab countries. This unsuccessful attempt by Qasim to acquire Kuwait further weakened his reputation within the Iraqi army and his authority as leader of Iraq.

In spite of his disfavor within the army, Qasim became popular

A July 1958 coup toppled the Iraqi monarchy and brought Colonel Abd al-Salam Arif (left) and General Abd al-Karim Qasim (right) to power. The two soon had a falling-out, however, and Qasim ordered his rival arrested.

with the Iraqi people because of his many reforms that helped the lower classes. He improved education and health care and began a land reform program that gave poor people farms of 20 to 40 acres.

However, Qasim allowed no representative government and became more and more dictatorial. His harsh policies caused many political groups to meet secretly. By the early 1960s, the Baathists had infiltrated the Qasim government and were able to enlist many civilians and army officers into their party.

But it was the continued dissatisfaction of Iraq's Kurdish population that ultimately undermined Qasim's dictatorship. The Kurds had supported the 1958 overthrow of the monarchy; in exchange Qasim had promised the Kurds a measure of equality with the Arab Iraqis. This never materialized, and by September 1961 the Kurds rose up against the Qasim government. Qasim ordered the bombing of Kurdish villages.

The Kurds asked the Baath Party for help, promising to stop fighting if Qasim were removed from power. On February 8, 1963, military units loyal to the Baath Party assassinated an army officer who supported Qasim. After a day of fighting between the Baathist units and troops loyal to the government, Qasim was captured, brought before a military tribunal, and sentenced to death. Abd al-Salam Arif, who had been imprisoned by Qasim, was freed and named president.

After the overthrow of Qasim, no plan had been developed to put a new government into place. The first action of the Baath Party's leaders was to eliminate Qasim's supporters and try to solidify their own position. Almost 3,000 were killed in the fighting that followed. The National Guard of the Baath Party, a military force that had grown to 30,000 men, carried out attacks against those the party's leaders felt were not in complete agreement with Baathist beliefs. The Guard arrested and tortured many innocent people. The Baath Party seemed especially determined to take the Kurdish territory and its wealth of oil. They bombed some Kurdish villages and demolished others with tanks, killing hundreds of Kurds.

This repression turned many Iraqis against the Baath Party. On November 18, 1963, President Arif ordered the military to attack the Baath National Guard in Baghdad, in order to solidify his own control over the country. To protect his government against further coups, Arif formed the Republican Guard from members of his own clan, stationing them around the city of Baghdad. Then he purged the government of its Baathist members.

Less than three years later, in April 1966, President Arif died in a helicopter crash, and his brother, General Abd al-Rahman Arif, became president. The new leader arranged a cease-fire with the Kurds. He also permitted the people of Iraq more freedom than they had enjoyed under any government since the overthrow of the monarchy. However, in 1966 the Baath Party was renewed under the leadership of General Ahmed Hassan al-Bakr, who appointed his cousin Saddam Hussein deputy secretary-general of the Regional Command of the Baath Party.

In 1968 three key officers in the Iraqi army led a coup that overthrew Arif's government and sent Arif into exile. Hassan al-Bakr became the president of Iraq, and Abd al-Razzaq al-Nayif, one of the three coup leaders, became prime minister.

The Baath Party learned from its mistakes of 1963. When the party seized power in 1968, it again did so with the help of military officers. However, soon after the coup the Baath leaders moved against the military. Al-Nayif was exiled, top officers were purged, and key Baath Party members were installed in the leadership positions. To inspire fear in anyone who might oppose his rule, Hassan al-Bakr ordered some of his opponents hanged in the streets of Baghdad. Saddam Hussein was placed in charge of the Baath Party's militia, and he showed no mercy when dealing with dissidents.

In 1972 Iraq nationalized its oil fields—meaning that revenue

Abd al-Rahman Arif, who assumed the presidency in 1966, relaxed government restrictions on personal freedom and arranged a cease-fire with the Kurds. But within two years his regime was overthrown by the socialist Baath Party.

from Iraqi petroleum production would no longer be split with foreign companies managing the oil fields. The foreign companies had received half of the profits. As a result, a torrent of money flowed to al-Bakr's government. By 1975 Iraq was earning some $8 billion a year from the sale of oil.

This wealth enabled the Baathist government not only to build up the military, but also to pour money into health care and education. Baghdad went through a building boom and turned from a dusty town of mud-brick houses into a modern city of high-rises.

But al-Bakr faced several problems as he and his associates tried to reinforce their hold on the government. Iran had often fought with Iraq over their common border on the Shatt al Arab, and in the early 1970s Iran was once again insisting that the border between the two countries should lie in the center of the waterway. This change would give Iran more control over the Shatt al Arab. The problem of dissident Kurds fighting for their freedom also continued. In 1969 Kurds had attacked the government's oil refinery at Kirkuk. After this the government of Iran, seeing an opportunity to harass Iraq, began to supply Kurdish guerrillas with weapons. By 1974 a full-scale war existed between the Iraqi government and the Kurds, who controlled the mountainous areas in the north.

In March of 1975, Iraq and Iran settled the Shatt al Arab issue. Iran received the border it wanted; in return, the **shah** agreed to stop supporting the Kurds. Without weapons and an escape route into Iran, Kurdish resistance evaporated. To prevent further rebellions, the Iraqi government literally yanked more than 50,000 Kurds from their homes and moved them into empty areas, giving them tents to live in. They were threatened with death if they tried to return to the Kurdistan region. Al-Bakr's government then encouraged Arab Iraqis to move into the former homes of the Kurds in order to dilute the influence of the Kurdish population.

By the end of 1975, Saddam Hussein had clearly become one of the most powerful men in Iraq. While al-Bakr was considered the more respectable face of the government, he had become little more than a figurehead. Saddam was the regime's strongman, intimidating Iraqis to ensure that no one opposed the Baath Party. Political activity among civilians or within the army, aside from that connected to the Baath Party, was outlawed and could be punished by death.

SADDAM HUSSEIN TAKES POWER

In July 1979 Saddam Hussein, then vice president of Iraq, announced that he had discovered a plot to take over the government. Among the plotters, he claimed, were high-ranking members of Iraq's government; not only were they "traitors" to their friends,

Saddam said, but they also were closely allied with Syria. Over the next two weeks, dozens of government officials and accused traitors were executed. President al-Bakr quietly slipped from the political scene, claiming ill health.

Saddam's authority soon became total. The people who were loyal to him were promoted to powerful positions in the government. In exchange, they agreed with him and supported his power grab. Saddam's most trusted officials were those who came from his hometown, Tikrit, and were members of his own family or tribe.

Saddam dealt strongly with any opposition. When Shiite Muslim religious leaders in southern Iraq encouraged resistance to the government, Saddam had some leading clerics killed and many others arrested. He accused numerous Shiites of supporting Iraq's rival, Iran, and thousands were forced to leave the country and move into Iran. After their deportation, their homes and belongings were sold.

Saddam had reason to be concerned about affairs in Iran. The pro-Western government of the shah had been overthrown in early 1979 by supporters of the radical Shiite cleric Ayatollah Ruhollah Khomeini. Khomeini had instituted a theocratic Shiite Muslim government. In the wake of Iran's Islamic Revolution, he encouraged Shiites in other countries to revolt against their leaders. Saddam Hussein's concern about the loyalty of his own Shiite population was warranted—he had ruthlessly oppressed the Shiites. Even before the Baath Party came to power, however, Shiites had been second-class citizens in Iraq, and they resented repression by the country's secular governments.

The Sunni-Shiite split was not the only dimension to the animosity between Iran and Iraq. The people of Mesopotamia had been at odds with the many Persian peoples to their east for millennia. And there was a personal element as well—Khomeini hated Saddam Hussein and his secular regime, while Saddam detested the ayatollah and his theocratic rule. Perhaps most important,

Saddam Hussein rose through the ranks of the Baath Party, finally seizing absolute power in July 1979 with a chilling, videotaped purge of party members.

though, was Saddam's desire to make Iraq the leading power in the Middle East, which would require that it overcome its larger rival Iran. The Islamic Revolution had caused great unrest in Iran, and Saddam wanted to exploit what he perceived as a strategic moment of Iranian weakness.

He used the long-running Shatt al Arab dispute as an excuse to start a war. In September 1980, Saddam announced Iraq's claim to the entire waterway, and within a few days Iraqi troops had invaded Iran and captured some territory.

The Iran-Iraq War lasted for eight years, during which time neither side was able to make permanent or significant gains. Instead, the war devastated both countries. Each bombed the other's oil refineries; Iraq's oil revenues fell from $26 billion in 1980 to $9 billion in 1982. To pay for the war, Saddam borrowed billions of dollars from Arab countries, particularly Kuwait and Saudi Arabia.

The United States also provided crucial support to Iraq throughout the war. Under Khomeini's leadership Iran had become the mortal enemy of the United States, and President Ronald Reagan feared that if Iran defeated Iraq, the Islamic Revolution would spread into the Arab world. This might cut off access to the oil reserves of the Persian Gulf, which the Western economies needed. As a result, the U.S. government provided financial aid and training to the Iraqis, as well as information on Iranian military positions. (However, during the later years of the war, the Reagan administration arranged secret shipments of weapons to Iran, in exchange for Tehran's cooperation in freeing Western hostages being held in Lebanon by Iranian-supported groups.)

The Iran-Iraq War was an uncommonly merciless conflict, producing casualties estimated at more than a million people—and the two countries' combined population was under 80 million. But beyond the massive casualties, there was another disturbing development: the use of chemical weapons. In violation of the 1925 Geneva Protocol on the Use of Chemical Weapons—to which Iraq was a signatory—Saddam's forces on various occasions resorted to chemical warfare against their Iranian enemies. A 1986 report from the United Nations documented Iraq's use of the banned weapons, such as mustard gas and nerve gas; a separate British report released later that year estimated that at least 10,000 Iranian soldiers had been killed in Iraqi chemical attacks.

But Iraq's use of chemical warfare was not limited to attacks on enemy soldiers. In March 1988, a chemical attack by Saddam's forces killed some 5,000 Kurdish civilians in the village of Halabja. At the time, the Iraqis were recapturing Kurdish territory in northeastern Iraq that had been occupied by Iranian troops.

The Halabja massacre was only the most famous chemical attack on the Kurds; there were many others. The Kurds, who had always resisted the government of Iraq, had supported Iran's invasion of northern Iraq. After the Iranian army was forced from Iraq, Saddam enacted a brutal campaign against the entire Kurdish population. Any Kurd thought to be a guerrilla or a supporter of Iran was killed. Villages were totally destroyed and their survivors sent to camps set up by the government. Mustard gas and nerve gas were used on 67 Kurdish villages. Many of those who survived the gas attacks were badly injured and horribly deformed, and the countryside was seriously contaminated. In all, it is believed that 80 percent of the villages in the Kurdish area were destroyed and 60,000 people killed in this purge.

After eight long years, the Iran-Iraq War finally ended in August 1988 with a United Nations–sponsored cease-fire. Though Iran had sustained heavier casualties, Iraq, too, was devastated by the war its leader had started. Approximately 375,000 Iraqis had been killed or wounded, and 60,000 more had been captured. Economic losses were also staggering: cities, oil fields, and refineries had been wrecked, and many areas of the country were in ruins. By the end of the war Iraq owed about $80 billion, mostly to its Arab neighbors.

 ## Text-Dependent Questions

1. What political party gained power in Iraq during the 1960s? What are some of the things the party supported?
2. When did Saddam Hussein become president of Iraq?
3. What was the outcome of the Iran-Iraq War?

 ## Research Project

Chemical weapons use toxic chemicals to incapacitate, harm, or kill others. They can be dispersed in gas, liquid, or solid forms. Due to their nature, chemical weapons often affect people other than their intended targets, and are considered weapons of mass destruction. They have been banned by many international treaties, most recently the 1993 Chemical Weapons Convention. Using the Internet or your school library, do some research on the two main types of chemical weapons (nerve agents and vesicant agents). What are the effects of each of these types of weapons? How large of an area or population can they effect?Write a two-page report, and include details about notable uses of these weapons in Iraq or elsewhere.

U.S. soldier William Highsmith sits with a young Iraqi boy outside a Baghdad clinic where members of the First Armored Division and Iraqi medical professionals are teaching a class in preventive medicine. The task of rebuilding Iraq after the war's end in April 2003 proved harder than most people expected.

Iraq at War and Rebuilding

In the period immediately after the Iran-Iraq War ended, roughly half of Iraq's oil revenues were spent just to repay the country's war debt. Because Saddam needed huge amounts of money to rebuild his country, he turned to the Organization of Petroleum Exporting Countries (OPEC) for help. OPEC is a **cartel** made up of developing countries that are among the largest global exporters of oil. It attempts to manage world oil prices by setting production quotas for its members, in order to control the amount of oil available for sale and keep prices at a high level. In 1989 Saddam asked OPEC to grant Iraq a larger annual quota. Pumping more oil would enable Iraq to bring in more income, which would help the country recover financially. When OPEC refused Saddam's request, Iraq's leader demanded that Saudi Arabia and Kuwait cancel their debts. The dictator argued that his war with Iran had been waged to defend the Arab world, and that because they had benefitted, they should participate in the cost. Both Saudi Arabia and Kuwait balked.

Saddam soon claimed that Kuwait was exceeding its OPEC quota, thereby lowering the international price of oil. He also said that Kuwait was pumping oil from a field under Iraq's border. The dictator used these claims as a pretext to invade Kuwait on August 2, 1990. In less than a week, Saddam declared Kuwait the 19th province of Iraq. The annexation of Kuwait would give Iraq greater access to the Persian Gulf, as well as control over Kuwait's extensive oil fields.

The international community refused to accept the Iraqi takeover. To oppose Iraq's aggression, the United States took the lead in building an international military coalition of more than 30 countries, and the United Nations demanded that Iraq withdraw its forces from Kuwait by January 15, 1991. The day after this deadline had passed with Iraqi troops still in Kuwait, Operation Desert Storm began with a campaign of aerial bombardment. After coalition warplanes bombed strategic targets in Iraq and Kuwait for several weeks, a multinational ground force, composed mainly of U.S. and British troops, moved into Kuwait.

The Gulf War was relatively brief, and decidedly one-sided: Saddam's army was routed after 100 hours of ground fighting. By the end of February, Iraqi soldiers were fleeing Kuwait, although hundreds were killed along a stretch of road between the two coun-

 Words to Understand in This Chapter

cartel—an association that attempts to maintain prices of a particular commodity a high level and restricting competition by managing the available supply of that commodity.

weapons of mass destruction—a term that refers to chemical, biological, and nuclear weapons, which are capable of causing many deaths each time they are used.

tries that became known as the "highway of death." As defeated Iraqi troops retreated from Kuwait, they left a trail of devastation, setting fire to oil fields, looting homes, and destroying public buildings and infrastructure. The rebuilding of Kuwait would cost some $160 billion. On February 28, 1991, with the goal of liberating Kuwait achieved, the United States unilaterally declared a ceasefire. The coalition's leaders did not want to pursue the Iraqi Army into Iraq, in part because they believed that some key allies, including Saudi Arabia and Turkey, would not support an effort to remove Saddam Hussein from power. However, U.S. President George H.W. Bush encouraged Iraqis to rise up and overthrow the dictator

Encouraged by Bush's words, in the aftermath of the Gulf War Shiite Muslims in the south and Kurds in the north rebelled against Saddam's regime. In Shiite cities like Basra and Karbala, returning

President George Bush greets U.S. troops in Saudi Arabia after the 1991 Gulf War. Although the brief war succeeded in expelling Iraq from Kuwait, it left Saddam Hussein in power.

soldiers and Shiite civilians attacked government officials. If the rebels believed President Bush's call to overthrow Saddam meant that the United States would help them, however, they were wrong. Despite his colossal defeat in the Gulf War, Saddam had managed to preserve his best-trained and most loyal military force, the elite Republican Guard. The dictator sent Republican Guard units south to recapture the cities and put down the revolt. Thousands of

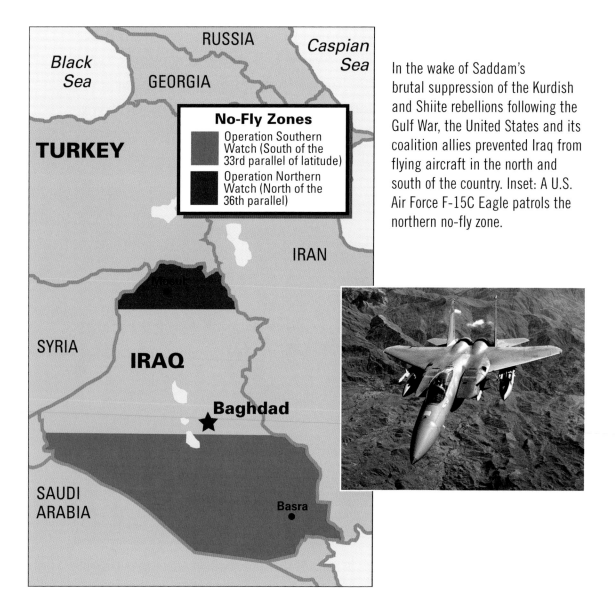

No-Fly Zones

Operation Southern Watch (South of the 33rd parallel of latitude)

Operation Northern Watch (North of the 36th parallel)

In the wake of Saddam's brutal suppression of the Kurdish and Shiite rebellions following the Gulf War, the United States and its coalition allies prevented Iraq from flying aircraft in the north and south of the country. Inset: A U.S. Air Force F-15C Eagle patrols the northern no-fly zone.

Shiites were killed, and many more fled to Iran or to refugee camps set up by the U.S. military.

Next, the Republican Guard moved north to attack the Kurds. As Saddam's troops brutally crushed the Kurdish uprising, more than a million Kurds fled their homes and headed toward Turkey or Iran. These refugees faced harsh conditions, including scant supplies of food and water and inadequate shelter against the late-winter cold of Iraq's rugged mountains. Refugees began to die, and a massive humanitarian crisis loomed.

After a period of hesitation, the United States, Britain, and France finally took action to protect the Kurds, setting up safe havens and declaring that no Iraqi aircraft would be permitted to fly north of the 36th parallel of latitude. This prevented Saddam's forces from using attack helicopters against the Kurds. A similar no-fly zone was later established south of the 33rd parallel, to give the Shiites a measure of protection.

Protected from attack by U.S. and British fighter-jet patrols—which enforced the no-fly zone from 1991 until 2003—Kurds who had fled returned to their homes. The Kurds were even able to create an autonomous region in northern Iraq, where they enjoyed political freedom unknown in the rest of the country. Free elections were held in May of 1992, and, in June of that year, an elected Kurdish Assembly convened for the first time.

THE EFFORT TO DISARM IRAQ

As part of the cease-fire that ended the 1991 Gulf War, Iraq agreed to obey United Nations resolutions demanding that it recognize the sovereignty of Kuwait and destroy its ***weapons of mass destruction***. In addition to chemical weapons—which it had used during the war with Iran—Iraq had produced biological weapons, including munitions filled with concentrated anthrax and botulinum toxin. Even more alarming was Iraq's nuclear weapons program. Although it had signed the 1968 Treaty on the Non-Proliferation of Nuclear Weapons, Iraq had secretly been working on a nuclear bomb, perhaps since the 1970s. Experts believed that by 1991 Iraq was just a few years away from becoming a nuclear power.

In early June of 1991, the United Nations Special Commission on Disarmament (UNSCOM) began searching Iraq for weapons of mass destruction. UNSCOM inspectors found and destroyed chemical weapons and proscribed missiles. They also concluded that Saddam's scientists had been considerably closer to developing nuclear weapons than Western intelligence analysts had suspected.

By late 1994, UNSCOM believed it was close to finishing its work. However, rumors emerged that Iraq had an undeclared biological weapons program, something that the country's leaders acknowledged in July 1995. The next month, Saddam's son-in-law, Hussein Kamel, who had been in charge of Iraq's proscribed weapons programs, defected. As a result of Kamel's defection, UNSCOM learned that Iraq had retained significant amounts of chemical agents, along with some missiles and other delivery systems. Iraq, however, never turned over any of that material. The Iraqis claimed they had destroyed it unilaterally, even though the U.N. cease-fire resolution called for UNSCOM to supervise destruction of that material.

Short of another full-scale war to remove Saddam Hussein from power—a course of action that lacked broad international support—the options for convincing Iraq to disarm were fairly limited. One option was the periodic bombing of selected targets. Another was continuation of the economic sanctions that the U.N. had imposed after Iraq's invasion of Kuwait. It was believed that restricting Iraq's trade with other countries would not only pressure Saddam to comply with the disarmament requirements, but also, if he resisted, limit his ability to rebuild his military and weapons programs.

Because Iraqi compliance was judged to be insufficient, the sanctions remained in effect throughout the 1990s. Some world leaders found this troubling, because while Saddam's regime continued to enjoy sufficient resources to maintain its hold on power, ordinary Iraqis suffered terribly. Shortages of food and medicine caused misery and death. In response to this situation, the United Nations in 1995 established the oil-for-food program, which permitted Iraq to sell oil under U.N. supervision; most of the profits were supposed to go to the humanitarian needs of Iraq's people. But, by most accounts, the regime managed to divert oil-for-food money for its own use, and Iraqis continued to suffer. Corruption was also later uncovered in the United Nations administration of the program, as well.

UNSCOM inspectors examine 155-mm artillery projectiles capable of carrying mustard gas at a facility in Fallujah, August 1991. Concern that Saddam Hussein was not fully complying with the United Nations Security Council resolution to end his WMD programs led to the implementation of economic sanctions throughout the 1990s and early 2000s.

Throughout the 1990s, Saddam Hussein bedeviled U.S. policy-makers. President Bill Clinton, who took office in 1993, pursued a policy of containment. The hope was that if Saddam could not be removed, he could at least be isolated and held in check through continued application of the economic sanctions. On occasion, however, the Clinton administration resorted to air strikes on Iraq. In June 1993, for example, President Clinton ordered a cruise missile attack on the office of Iraq's intelligence agency in Baghdad following revelations of an Iraqi plot to assassinate his predecessor, George Bush. Saddam's moves against the opposition Iraqi National Congress in 1996 provoked another cruise missile strike.

But for U.S. policymakers, uncertainty about Iraq's weapons programs was the greatest concern. At different times throughout 1996 and 1997, efforts by UNSCOM inspectors to inspect various sites in Iraq were blocked or delayed, resulting in several U.N. declarations of noncompliance with security council resolutions. In September 1998, Saddam Hussein demanded that American members of UNSCOM had to leave the country, accusing them of spying. In response the United Nations withdrew the entire team, and President Clinton sent U.S. Navy warships into the Persian Gulf, threatening Iraq with air strikes. Cornered, Saddam permitted the inspectors to return.

The dictator used many methods to frustrate UNSCOM's inspection efforts. Saddam declared his presidential palaces—some of which were huge compounds where just about anything could be hidden—off-limits to inspectors. He refused to allow UNSCOM to return to sites it had previously inspected. UNSCOM was prohibited from searching the headquarters of the Baath Party in Baghdad.

In December 1998, with military action against Iraq imminent, the United Nations withdrew its inspectors. The United States and Great Britain then began Operation Desert Fox, a bombing campaign to force Saddam to comply with the U.N. resolutions. During

President George W. Bush (left) and Secretary of Defense Donald Rumsfeld, two of the architects of the war to topple Saddam Hussein, hoped that the establishment of a democratic Iraq would lead to wide-ranging reforms among the Arab regimes of the Middle East.

the three-day operation, missiles were fired at strategic Iraqi military targets and suspected weapons sites. However, U.N. inspectors were not permitted to return to Iraq after this attack.

In the aftermath of the September 11, 2001, terrorist attacks against the United States, the U.S. government revised its policy toward Iraq, replacing "containment" with "regime change." President George W. Bush, who had taken office in January 2001, and key members of his administration argued that the United Nations would become "irrelevant" if it did not respond to Saddam Hussein's flouting of its many resolutions regarding disarmament.

In November 2002, the United Nations Security Council voted unanimously to adopt Resolution 1441. The resolution gave Iraq "a

U.S. soldiers observe a burning oil well at the Rumaylah oilfield in southern Iraq, April 2003.

final opportunity to comply with its disarmament obligations" and warned of "serious consequences" if it did not do so. Faced with the prospect of war, Saddam permitted U.N. weapons inspectors to return to Iraq in December.

Over the next few months, the Bush administration pressured other governments to find that Iraq was still in "material breach" of its obligations under Resolution 1441. Many countries, such as France, Germany, Russia, and China, resisted. Nevertheless, on March 20, 2003, the United States and Great Britain began a war to drive Saddam Hussein from power. By April 9, American troops had swept into Baghdad, and Saddam was in hiding. It was apparent that the Iraqi regime had collapsed. On May 1, just six weeks after the start of the war, President Bush announced the end of "major combat operations."

THE AFTERMATH OF WAR

The collapse of Saddam Hussein's government occurred so quickly that U.S. forces were not prepared to step in immediately and maintain order. People throughout Iraq celebrated the fall of the regime on April 9, 2003, but celebrations soon turned into rioting in Baghdad and other cities. Unrest in the capital prevented Red Cross workers from delivering medical supplies and fresh water to hospitals. U.S. troops concentrated on eliminating military resistance, but they did not prevent looters from stealing priceless archaeological treasures from museums and libraries in Baghdad, robbing banks and government buildings in Basra, or plundering the university in Mosul. Soon, crowds began to gather to protest the U.S. occupation of Iraq. In many cases, Muslim religious leaders, both Sunni and Shiite, incited the protesters.

Attacks on U.S. troops continued after President Bush declared an end to major combat operations in Iraq on May 1. Sunni Muslim insurgents determined to resist the U.S. occupation waged a bloody guerrilla campaign of suicide bombings and ambushes. The Sunni

U.S. soldiers take inventory of weapons found hidden in Thalatat, Iraq, November 2003. In the months that followed the war, an Iraqi resistance to the U.S. occupation inflicted many casualties on coalition troops.

insurgency was fueled in large part by the decision of the Coalition Provisional Authority (CPA)—the transitional government set up by the U.S. after the overthrow of Saddam Hussein—to dismiss Iraq's army and ban former members of the Baath Party from holding government jobs.

The insurgents, often led by former Baath Party members, targeted U.S. forces as well as Iraqi Shiites. Shiites retaliated, carrying out murderous violence against their Sunni neighbors. Shiite militias also battled American soldiers. In addition, foreign fighters—some linked to the terrorist organization al-Qaeda—slipped into Iraq and carried out indiscriminate attacks against civilians. They hoped to foment a civil war and thereby make Iraq ungovernable.

As the insurgency continued, the CPA and the Bush administration were blamed for the many problems that occurred during the reconstruction process. Electrical power was spotty in many places, and people had to wait in long lines for food, clean water, gasoline, and other necessities. The CPA pointed to its accomplishments—rebuilding schools and hospitals; connecting water, power, and telephone lines; clearing harbors and canals; and other projects. However, the slow pace of reconstruction angered many Iraqis and fueled protests against the U.S. occupation. In the United States, meanwhile, critics complained that the Bush administration had created a detailed plan to win the war, but it had done scant prewar planning of how to rebuild Iraq.

The administration was also widely criticized because its inspectors had not turned up evidence that Saddam Hussein possessed weapons of mass destruction—the original rationale for invading Iraq. In June of 2003, a U.S. organization called the Iraq Survey Group (ISG) took over the task of looking for the banned weapons. In October, the ISG issued a preliminary report and its leader, former U.N. chief weapons inspector Dr. David Kay, told the U.S. Senate that no stocks of prohibited chemical, biological, or nuclear

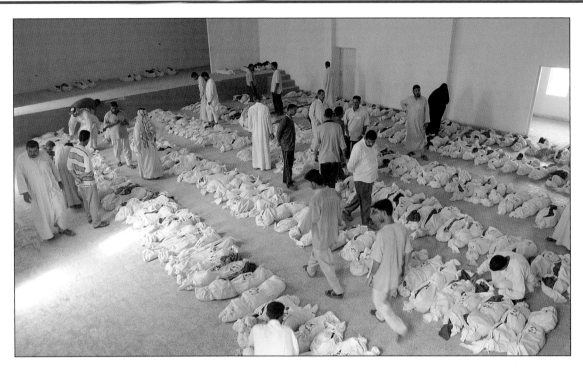

Iraqis search for their relatives and friends among the remains of victims found in a mass grave in Musayib, about 47 miles (75 km) southwest of Baghdad. After the fall of Saddam Hussein, human-rights officials estimated that more than 300,000 Iraqis had been murdered during the dictator's reign.

weapons had been found, despite months of intensive searching. However, the report said that the ISG had discovered dozens of WMD-related activities and significant amounts of equipment concealed from U.N. inspectors between 1991 and 1998, including a secret network of laboratories suitable for WMD research and a vial containing a potential biological warfare agent hidden in a scientist's home. There was no evidence that Iraq had tried to build nuclear weapons after 1998, although there was evidence that Saddam had tried to acquire the weapons.

Although the suspected weapons of mass destruction were not found, plenty of evidence demonstrated the brutality of Saddam Hussein's regime. Research by the CPA and non-governmental organizations turned up more than 250 mass graves throughout the country, The grave sites contained the remains of at least 300,000 murdered Iraqis. Most of the victims were believed to be Kurds, Shiites, or opponents of Saddam's regime or the Baath Party.

Saddam himself was finally captured on December 13, 2003, when U.S. soldiers found him hiding in a tiny tunnel on a farm in Adwar, a town about 10 miles (16 km) from his hometown of Tikrit. In July 2004, Saddam and a number of his top aids were arraigned by the Iraqi Special War Crimes Tribunal. The charges against him included: the arrest and execution of religious figures between 1974 and 1984; the murder of the Kurdish Barzani clan in 1983; the 1986–88 Anfal campaign against the Kurds; the gassing of Halabja in 1988; the 1990 invasion of Kuwait; and the suppression of uprisings by Kurds and Shiites in 1991.

In October 2005, Saddam and seven associates went on trial in an Iraqi court for crimes against humanity. The charges stemmed from the 1982 killing of nearly 150 Shiites in Dujail, a town north of Baghdad where an attempt to assassinate Saddam had been made. After a yearlong trial, Saddam was found guilty and sentenced to death. On December 30, 2006, the former dictator of Iraq was hanged.

FIGHTING THE INSURGENCY

American troops suffered thousands of casualties trying to bring order to Iraq. Bush administration officials and the CPA hoped that elections and the handover of the government to Iraqis would stanch the violence. In January 2005, Iraqis voted for a transitional national assembly. In December of that year, following the adoption of a constitution, Iraqis went to the polls and voted for a permanent government.

Unfortunately, hopes that the elections would bring peace were soon dashed. Violence remained high throughout 2005. And in February 2006, a deadly attack on an important Shiite shrine in

Iraqi Police and U.S. Marines watch a line of Iraqi citizens waiting to cast their ballots at a polling station in Fallujah during Iraq's historic election in January 2005.

Samarra unleashed an even more brutal wave of sectarian killing. By the end of 2006, according to the United Nations, more than 34,000 Iraqi civilians had been killed. The country threatened to spiral into complete chaos.

There were some positive signs by the end of that year, however. In late 2006, Sunni leaders in the western province of Anbar had decided to stop fighting American forces. In return for monthly cash payments, the Iraqi Sunnis joined American soldiers in fighting foreign terrorists. This development, called the Awakening movement, gradually spread to other parts of Iraq.

In January 2007, the Bush administration announced a troop "surge." By September an additional 40,000 American soldiers had joined the 130,000 already in the country. Accompanying the surge was a shift in U.S. strategy, from focusing on traditional combat operations to focusing on counterinsurgency, including holding territory, providing jobs, and fostering reconstruction.

In August 2007 Moqtada al-Sadr, the leader of Iraq's largest Shiite militia, the Mehdi Army, announced a cease-fire. The combination of the Shiite cease-fire, the Sunni Awakening, and the shift in American military strategy contributed to decreased levels of violence in Iraq, and hope that the conflict was finally near an end. Still, the prospects for a peaceful and stable Iraq hinged on political compromises among the country's sectarian groups—which was by no means guaranteed.

By late 2008 the government of Prime Minister Nouri al-Maliki was confident enough in the progress toward stability to begin negotiating a security agreement with the United States by which all American troops would leave Iraq by the end of 2011. In early 2009 the newly elected U.S. president, Barack Obama, announced his intention to withdraw most American military forces from Iraq by August 2010, with all forces to be removed by 2011 in compliance with the Iraqi government's wishes. In December 2011 the last U.S. troops left the country and the war was declared over.

CONTINUING CONFLICT

Although the insurgency seemed to be under control, it would soon flare up again once the U.S. troops left Iraq. In part, this occurred due to outside events: the "Arab Spring" revolts and a civil war in neighboring Syria.

In late 2010 and early 2011, anti-government protests began to occur in a number of Arab countries. The protests—which became known as the Arab Spring—were aimed at improving the political circumstances and living conditions of the Arab people. In Syria, people began protesting against the Baath Party, which had ruled the country since the 1960s. Inspired by successful revolutions in Tunisia and Egypt, Syrian protesters used marches, hunger strikes, rioting, vandalism, and guerrilla attacks in an attempt to overthrow the government of President Bashar al-Assad. The Syrian uprising soon devolved into a full-blown civil war.

In Iraq, Arab Spring protests began in early 2012, as Sunni Muslims boycotted the Shiite-dominated government, claiming that it was trying to minimize Sunnis. In addition, both Iraqi Sunnis and Shiites were galvanized by the Syrian civil war, and many militants from both sects crossed the border to fight in Syria.

During 2013 Sunni militant groups increased their attacks, targeting the Iraq's Shia population in an attempt to undermine confidence in the government.

In 2014 Sunni insurgents belonging to the Islamic State of Iraq and the Levant (ISIL) terrorist group seized control of large swathes of land including several major Iraqi cities, like Tikrit, Fallujah and Mosul creating hundreds of thousands of internally displaced persons amid reports of atrocities by ISIL fighters.

 ## Text-Dependent Questions

1. What United Nations agency was responsible for making sure Iraq dismantled its WMD programs?
2. Where was Saddam Hussein captured? What happened to him?
3. What events helped to fuel the current conflict in Iraq that began in 2011?

 ## Research Project

In late 2010, sparked by the self-immolation of a fruit vendor in Tunisia, anti-government protests began to erupt throughout the Arab world. The ongoing protests are aimed at improving the political circumstances and living conditions of the Arab people, and have become known in the West as the "Arab Spring." Using your school library or the internet, find out more about the origin of the Arab Spring protests. Take a blank map of the Arab countries (one can be printed online from http://commons.wikimedia.org/wiki/File:Arab_world_location_map.svg). Label and mark the countries where protesters succeeded in overthrowing or changing governments.

Shiite Muslims walk past the mosque at the tomb of Hussain ibn Ali, a sacred shrine in Karbala. About 97 percent of Iraq's people are adherents of Islam, the majority belonging to the Shia branch of the faith.

Religion, Politics, and the Economy

It is impossible to understand Iraq without understanding the country's most important religion, Islam. The Islamic faith is a vital part of everything Iraqis do. Islam is the world's second-largest religion; there are more than a billion Muslims, and many of them live in the Middle East and Asia. In Iraq, almost 97 percent of the people are Muslim.

ISLAM

The name of this **monotheistic** religion, Islam, comes from the Arabic verb *aslama*, which means "to surrender." Muslims, or followers of Islam, are those who surrender to the will of Allah, who is considered the one true God. Muslims believe that in the seventh century CE, Allah spoke through the Angel Gabriel to Muhammad. Over a period of 22 years, the Prophet, as Muhammad is called, received Allah's messages and taught them to his followers. At first his disciples memorized them; they later wrote down the messages in a collection called the Qur'an (or Koran). The word *Qur'an* means "recitation" and comes from the Arabic word *iqira*, meaning "recite"—the first word that the Angel Gabriel spoke to Muhammad. Muslims believe the Qur'an is the perfect word of God.

Muslims are expected to follow five important precepts, or "pillars." The first is *shahada* ("testimony"), a prayer that expresses the belief at the heart of Islam: "There is no God but Allah, and Muhammad is the messenger of Allah." Devout Muslims recite the *shahada* each day. The second pillar is *salah* ("prayer"). Adult Muslims are required to pray five times during the day. The third pillar is *zakat* ("charity"), a donation given to people in need. The fourth pillar is *sawm* ("fasting"), a requirement that Muslims abstain from food, drink, and certain other activities during daylight hours of Ramadan, the ninth month of the lunar Islamic calendar. The fifth pillar is *hajj* ("pilgrimage"), a journey that Muslims who are physically and financially able must make to Mecca and other important Islamic sites at least once during their lifetime.

There are many sects of Islam, although the major split is between the Sunni Muslims and the Shiite Muslims. This division occurred more than 1,300 years ago, and the area of Iraq was a key battleground as Sunnis and Shiites fought for control of the religion. Today, it is estimated that more than 80 percent of the world's Muslims are Sunnis, while about 15 percent are Shiites. Iraq is one

Words to Understand in This Chapter

monotheistic—believing in the existence of only one God.
salinity—the level of salt in water or soil.

of just a few countries where the Shiite population is larger than the Sunni population. (Other Middle Eastern countries with more Shiites than Sunnis include Iran, Lebanon, and Bahrain.) According to recent figures, between 60 and 65 percent of Iraq's population are Shiites, while 32 to 37 percent are Sunnis. Despite the Shiites' majority status, since the time of the Ottoman Empire Sunni Muslims have traditionally held the power in Iraq.

In addition to the Qur'an, Muslims believe that the *hadiths* (sayings of the Prophet) are very important. The *hadiths* and stories about Muhammad are collected in the *Sunna* (traditions of the Prophet). Over the years, the Qur'an and the *Sunna* have given rise to a number of religious laws and codes of conduct; Islamic law is known as *Sharia*. In many Muslim countries of the Middle East, *Sharia* forms the basis not just for the justice system but also for legislation. While Iraq during the rule of Saddam Hussein had some special religious courts whose decisions were based on *Sharia*, the Baath Party was a secular organization, and Islam was not the foundation of the country's laws or justice system. (Unfortunately, legislation and the justice system were all too often simply tools for Saddam's regime to maintain its grip on power.)

OTHER RELIGIONS IN IRAQ

Although the overwhelming majority of Iraqis—both Arabs and Kurds—follow Islam, Iraq also has a small Christian community. Ancestors of these people have lived in Iraq for nearly 2,000 years. The Assyrians live in the northern part of Iraq, near the Kurdish enclaves that were protected by the northern no-fly zone between 1991 and 2003. Assyrians are a separate ethnic group from Kurds and Arabs. They still speak a version of Aramaic, the ancient language of the Middle East that was supplanted by Arabic during the spread of Islam in the seventh and eighth centuries. Historically, the Assyrians have been subject to repression by Iraqi rulers, and in recent years there have been some incidents of violence between Kurdish Muslims and Assyrian Christians. The Assyrian Christian population in Iraq is estimated at between 600,000 and 1 million.

THE GOVERNMENT OF IRAQ

Following the overthrow of Saddam Hussein's regime in April 2003, the Bush administration hoped to establish a democratic government in Iraq. After several attempts, an Iraqi Governing Council was established, with 25 members representing Iraq's various sectarian groups. The Governing Council's powers were very limited, however. In addition, because its members were chosen by U.S. authorities in the Coalition Provisional Authority (CPA), the Governing Council never gained the trust of the Iraqi people.

In March 2004 the Governing Council passed an interim constitution, which paved the way for the announcement of an interim prime minister the following month. In June the CPA formally transferred authority to Iraq's interim government, which was headed by Prime Minister Iyad Allawi, a Shiite. A Sunni was chosen for the largely ceremonial post of interim president.

In January 2005, Iraqis voted for members of the Transitional National Assembly. The United Iraqi Alliance, a Shiite party, won the most seats. Kurdish parties also made a strong showing, largely because most Sunnis boycotted the election. A new constitution—which was supposed to create a federal democracy—was approved in October 2005.

In elections held in December to select members of a permanent parliament, called the Council of Representatives, the United Iraqi Alliance again came out on top. Still, it did not gain a majority of seats, and while Iraq was being torn apart by sectarian violence, months of political gridlock ensued. Finally, a government was formed under Nouri al-Maliki of the Shiite Dawa Party.

In Iraq's current government, the president is the head of state, and performs many ceremonial duties. The president is elected by the members of the Council of Representatives. A Kurdish politician, Jalal Talabani, served as president of Iraq from April 2005 to July 2014. Talabani was succeeded by another Kurd, Fuad Masum.

One of the president's most important duties is to select the prime minister, who actually runs the day-to-day operations of Iraq's government and is the leader of the Council of Representatives. The Shiite politician Nouri al-Maliki became prime minister in 2005, but he was often criticized during his tenure for discriminating against Sunni Arabs. In August 2014, during the Islamic State crisis, Maliki resigned the post of prime minister under pressure from President Masum. He was succeeded by Haider al-Abadi, also a Shia Muslim.

The Council of Representatives currently includes 328 members. The Council meets in Baghdad for two sessions each year, during which it passes national laws,

Traditionally, Kurds have held the office of presidency, while Shiites have held the post of prime minister, to ensure balance among those factions. Iraq's current president, Fuad Masum, helped to draft the country's constitution.

In August of 2014, Haider al-Abadi became prime minister of Iraq. The prime minister is permitted to serve two four-year terms.

ratifies treaties, and approves the nomination of certain high-ranking government officials.

THE ECONOMY OF IRAQ

The production of oil is the most important part of Iraq's economy. Iraq has an estimated 140 billion barrels of proven oil reserves, giving it the fifth-largest reserves of any country in the world. The oil flows from 70 oil fields throughout the country, from Kirkuk in the northeast to Basra in the south.

Iraq has nine oil refineries. The two largest are in central Iraq—one at Bayji, which is north of Baghdad, and another, called Dawrah, in Baghdad.

Iraq fully nationalized the oil industry in 1975, and by 1979 it was producing 3.4 million barrels per day (bpd). Production dropped off during the Iran-Iraq War (1980–88), but by 1989 Iraq had rebuilt its extraction and refining capability and was nearly back to the 1979 production level.

After Iraq's invasion of Kuwait and the Gulf War, oil production fell to less than 600,000 bpd, due in large part to the United Nations sanctions against the country. As Iraq was permitted to export greater amounts of oil through the U.N.'s oil-for-food program, production gradually increased, officially reaching about 2 million bpd during 2001. The 2003 invasion by the U.S.-led coalition disrupted the oil industry again, but by 2009 Iraq's petroleum output was back around 2 million bpd.

After years of neglect, the infrastructure of Iraq's oil industry is old and prone to breakdowns. The World Bank

 Did You Know?

Some oil industry experts believe that a huge amount of oil—possibly as much as another 220 billion barrels—may still lie hidden beneath Iraq's sands. However, the unrest in the country over the past three decades has made new exploration nearly impossible.

has estimated that the country would have to invest billions of dollars to upgrade this infrastructure to maintain the current level of production. In 2009, the Iraqi Ministry of Oil granted licenses allowing international oil companies to access some of the country's oil fields, paying a royalty to the government. Some of those funds are being used to upgrade roads, pipelines, ports, and oil refining facilities. The balance is used by the government for other important infrastructure improvements, such as new schools, hospitals, and highways.

In addition to its vast oil resources, Iraq has 110 trillion cubic feet of proven natural gas reserves. Of that, 70 percent is "associated" natural gas, which is produced at the same time that oil is extracted.

There are three main manufacturing areas in Iraq, the most

An oil pumping station in southern Iraq. The country controls the world's fifth-largest petroleum reserves, and oil is an important part of Iraq's economy.

important of which is near Baghdad. Another one is at Basra, to the south of Baghdad. The third is in a triangle formed by the northern cities of Mosul, Erbil, and Kirkuk. Pharmaceuticals, paper and plastic products, household appliances, clothing, and automobiles are produced in all three regions. In addition, for generations Mosul has been an important textile center.

Although Mesopotamia is known as an early center of agriculture, farming plays only a small part in modern Iraq's economy, contributing just 6 percent to the country's gross domestic product. Only about 13 percent of Iraq is fit for growing crops, and about half of that land is in the Kurdish areas of the north and northeast, where rain waters the land. Most of the farm products are produced on the plains of central Iraq, where fields are watered by irriga-

Quick Facts: The Economy of Iraq

Gross domestic product (GDP*): $249.4 billion (rank 52nd in the world)
GDP per capita: $7,100 (rank 141st in the world)
GDP growth rate: 4.2% (rank 72nd in the world)
Inflation: 2% (rank 70th in the world)
Unemployment Rate: 16% (2012 est.) (rank 143rd in the world)
Natural resources: petroleum, natural gas, phosphates, sulfur
Agriculture (3.3% of GDP): wheat, barley, rice, vegetables, dates, cotton; cattle, sheep, poultry
Industry (64.6% of GDP): petroleum, chemicals, textiles, leather, construction materials, food processing, fertilizer, metal fabrication/processing
Services (32.1% of GDP): government, banking, other
Foreign trade:
    Imports—$66.61 billion: food, medicine, manufactures
    Exports—$91.99 billion: crude oil, raw materials, live animals
Currency exchange rate: 1,165 Iraqi dinars = U.S. $1 (2015)

*GDP, or gross domestic product, is the total value of goods and services produced in a country annually.
All figures are 2014 estimates unless otherwise noted.
Source: CIA World Factbook, 2015.

tion—just as they have been since the time of the Sumerians. This dependence on irrigation in the central region makes Turkish and Syrian water projects on the Euphrates River a very serious issue to the people of Iraq.

Another serious issue affecting agriculture in Iraq is **salinity**. The high water table in Iraq, the land's poor drainage, and the high rate of evaporation caused by the region's high temperatures cause salt to build up near the surface of the ground. The increasing salt level gradually makes it impossible to grow crops, turning the land into desert. Today, salinity affects almost two-thirds of Iraq, and it has caused once-productive land to be abandoned. In recent years, projects have been started to reclaim this land and make it useful again. However, this is a long, difficult process that requires consistent effort.

The major farm crops of Iraq include barley and wheat, which are grown during the winter, and cotton, potatoes, and millet, which are grown in the summer. Other summer crops include sorghum and tobacco. Dates and rice grow in the irrigated areas of the central plains along the rivers and canals.

Text-Dependent Questions

1. What is the largest Muslim sect in Iraq, Sunni or Shiite?
2. What Kurdish politician became president of Iraq in August 2014?
3. What natural resource is the most important part of Iraq's economy?

Research Project

To understand the importance of desalinization, watch this short video on the process at https://www.youtube.com/watch?v=2XMRIFMJB-g

Iraqi women walk through a market in Karbala. With respect to the status of women, Iraq has historically been liberal in comparison with other Arab countries. Iraq's current constitution guarantees women equal treatment with men under the law.

The People

Arab culture came to dominate Iraq after the Muslim conquests of the seventh and eighth centuries. Today, almost 8 in 10 of Iraq's approximately 32.5 million people are of Arab ancestry. Most of these Arabs are Shiite Muslims, who live predominantly in the southern or central parts of the country.

Iraq's second-largest ethnic group is its approximately 5.7 million Kurds, who make up about 15 to 20 percent of the population. Most of the Kurdish population is located in the northern part of Iraq. The Kurds' language and culture differs greatly from that of Arab Iraqis. Also, most of the Kurds are Sunni Muslims, unlike the Shiite Arab majority.

The Kurds have been called the largest ethnic group without their own state. There are estimated to be about 25 million Kurds worldwide; most of them live in an area known as Kurdistan, which includes parts of present-day Iraq, Iran, Turkey, and Syria. Since the early years of the 20th century, many Kurds have campaigned for their own independent state in this region. However, all of the governments that would be affected oppose giving up some of their territory for a Kurdish state.

After the 1991 Gulf War, the United States and Great Britain imposed a no-fly zone over northern Iraq to protect the Kurds from Saddam Hussein's armies. With this protection, Iraqi Kurdistan became a de facto democratic state during the 1990s; its people elected a lawmaking parliament, developed a system of government, and established an army and police force. Yet the Kurdistan model proved far from perfect. Two rival groups, the Kurdistan Democratic Party and the Patriotic Union of Kurdistan, battled for control. Their political fighting at times turned violent. Kurds have also attempted to terrorize and control the Assyrian Christian population living in the northern provinces of Iraq.

The Assyrians make up about 1 percent of Iraq's total population. Other ethnic groups living in the country include Turkomen, a nomadic Turkic people who live along the northern border of Iraq and make up about 1.4 percent of the total population. Armenians, Persians, and smaller groups together make up less than 2 percent

Words to Understand in This Chapter

calligraphy—artistic, elegant handwriting or lettering.

dialects—regional varieties of a language that are distinguished by differences in pronunciation, grammar, and vocabulary.

geometric—consisting of, or based on, shapes such as circles, squares, or straight lines.

patriarchal—relating to a social group in which the father is the supreme head, and wives and children are legally dependent upon him.

polygon—a closed figure on a sphere bounded by arcs of great circles.

plaintive—expressing suffering or woe.

Iraq's largest concentration of people is in Bagdad—home to nearly one in four Iraqis—and a narrow strip running southeast of the capital along the Tigris River. Few people live west of the Euphrates.

of Iraq's population. Many of these people have left Iraq for neighboring countries due to the unrest following the 2003 invasion, the ongoing civil war, or the conquests of the Islamic State.

Wars and sanctions have affected population growth in Iraq. During the 1980s, the country's population growth rate was 3.2 percent per year, but by the early 1990s the figure had slipped below 2 percent per year as the country's birth rate dropped. By

An Iraqi family outside their home. In Arab cultures, strong family ties are imperative.

2014 the population growth rate had risen to about 2.2 percent.

FAMILY LIFE IN IRAQ

The role of family in the Arab world helps explain much about the Arab Iraqi people. Kinship groups are the basic units in Iraqi society. Iraqis show their greatest loyalty to their immediate family and extended family. Usually three generations live together and share their lives, each having clear responsibilities. Other relatives live close by in the neighborhood. Often members of the same extended family are in business together because of the trust and powerful bond built up among them. A common proverb among Arabs is "I and my brothers against my cousin; I and my cousin against the stranger (or the world)."

One family is usually made up of an older couple, their sons, daughters-in-law, and their grandchildren. Traditionally, daughters remain in the home until they marry. Then they move into the home of their husband's family. Sometimes other relatives also might be a part of the household. The oldest male in that family is the head of the whole family and has the final word on all decisions. The father metes out the punishment, which can be severe, while the mother tends to offer the love and compassion. As in other Arab countries, Iraq's is a highly **patriarchal** society in which the male dominates, and male children are highly prized.

In spite of changing times, in many families the father decides the activities of the members under him, even determining what jobs his sons will have. Along with his wife, the father will pick out a husband for their daughter. Marriage is much more of a contract between two groups than the personal choice of two people, because the marriage will affect each of the families involved. Marriage is also still largely endogamous, especially outside large cities, which means a preference for cousin marriage. This tends to cement relations among clans and help provide order and self-defense in the traditional absence of centralized state authority.

Iraqis, like other Arabs, have a special love for the Arabic language. Since they believe the Qur'an represents the actual words of God, and since it was given to Muhammad in the Arabic language, it follows, then, that the original, classic Arabic is a divine language, according to devout Muslims. There are different Arabic **dialects**, however. Many say that Arabic can only be compared to music in the effect it has on those who speak and listen to it. In *The Arab Mind* Philip Hitti, a leading Arab-American histori-

 Did You Know?

The words *alcohol, algebra, admiral, elixir, gauze,* and *magazine* all come from the Arabic language.

an, was quoted as saying, "Hardly any language seems capable of exercising over the minds of its users such influence as Arabic. Modern audiences in Baghdad, Damascus and Cairo can be stirred to the highest degree by the recital of poems only vaguely comprehended, and by the delivery of orations in the classical tongue, though only partially understood."

Traditionally, Kurds have been organized by tribes, although tribal affiliation has become less important in recent years. Kurdish villages and cities have grown in the highlands and mountain valleys of northern Iraq, particularly in the three provinces of As Sulaymaniyah,

Quick Facts: The People of Iraq

Population: 32,585,692 (rank 40th in the world)
Ethnic groups: Arab, 75%–80%; Kurdish, 15%–20%; Turkomen, Assyrian, or other, 5%
Religions: Islam (official), 99% (Shia 60%–65%, Sunni 32%–37%); Christian, 0.8%; other, 0.2%
Language: Arabic (official); Kurdish (official); Turkmen (a Turkish dialect) and Assyrian (Neo-Aramaic) are official in areas where they constitute a majority of the population); Armenian
Age structure:
　0–14 years: 36.7%
　15–24 years: 19.6%
　25–54 years: 36.3%
　55–64 years: 4.2%
　65 years and over: 3.2%
Population growth rate: 2.23% (rank 42nd in the world)
Birth rate: 26.85 births/1,000 population (rank 46nd in the world)
Death rate: 4.57 deaths/1,000 population (rank 200th in the world)
Infant mortality rate: 37.53 deaths/ 1,000 live births (rank 62nd in the world)
Life expectancy at birth:
　total population: 71.42 years (rank 146th in the world)
　males: 69.93 years
　females: 72.99 years
Literacy: 78.5% (2011 est.)

All figures are 2014 estimates unless otherwise indicated.
Source: Adapted from CIA World Factbook, 2015.

Erbil, and Dahuk.

The Kurds have their own traditions and cultures. One source of pride that unifies Kurds is their language. In Iraqi Kurdistan, Kurdish, rather than in Arabic, has become the official language of schools and government.

THE ARTS

Islamic tradition forbids visual art in which Allah or living people are represented. As a result, throughout history Arab artists have expressed themselves through decorative art.

One art form popular in Iraq is **calligraphy**, writing so beautiful that it becomes a work of art in itself. Calligraphy—often sections of the Qur'an or Arab proverbs—can be used to decorate everyday items made from paper, metal, or wood. Sometimes the writing is so ornate that it is difficult to make out the exact words, and the calligraphy must be examined carefully in order to decipher the message.

Creating intricate **geometric** designs, often called arabesques, is another form of Iraqi art. The artist begins with a simple geometric form, such as a square, a circle, or a **polygon**, then uses this form to create complex patterns. Designs can be made with tile to decorate walls and doorways; colorful geometric designs can also be found on household items and clothing. Similar patterns, in which simple forms can be expanded into very complex but symmetrical works of art, can be discerned in architecture, music, and poetry.

Islamic architecture is another creative art form. Though the Arabs created palaces and other private buildings, the most lasting are the mosques. In Baghdad the celebrated Al-Kadhimain Mosque, built in the 16th century, has gold-capped domes and minarets rising above a courtyard.

Music is an important part of life in Iraq. Singers are accompanied by musical instruments such as the oud, which is something

Geometric motifs and calligraphy adorn this Islamic shrine in the Iraqi town of Al-Kufa. Such forms of decoration are common because Islam traditionally avoids the depiction of humans.

like a guitar. Iraqi musicians also play *darabukkas* (drums), *duffs* (tambourines), stringed instruments called *rabaabs*, the *qarna* (a horn), and the *zummara* (a double flute).

Traditional Iraqi music differs from American music in that it has only a melody, whereas Western music incorporates both melody and harmony. To a Westerner, this traditional Iraqi music is ***plaintive*** and squealing, while to many Iraqis Western music sounds crude and rough. However, younger Iraqis enjoy popular Western music.

Literature is an art form that has existed in Iraq since ancient times. One of the oldest writings in the world is the *Epic of Gilgamesh*, the story of an ancient Mesopotamian king's adventures.

Over the past two decades, many modern Iraqi artists have fled their country due to political persecution or to escape the violence. Poets and writers frequently have expressed their longing for Iraq in their work. One well-known author is Saadi Yousef, who currently lives in London and has published more than 30 books of poetry. The novelist and poet Fadhil Al Azzawi, who now lives in Germany, has won many awards for his work. Playwright Salah Al-Hamdani, now living in France, has criticized both Saddam Hussein and the United States in his plays.

Text-Dependent Questions

1. What percentage of Iraqis are Arabs? What percentage are Kurds?
2. In what region do the Turkomen people live?
3. What are some art forms that are popular in Iraq?

Research Project

Some contemporary Iraqis who are popular or well known include architect Zaha Hadid, singers Kadim al-Sahir and Dashni Murad, soccer players Ali Adnan and Ahmed Yasin Ghani, and new president Fuad Masum. Historical figures include the Medieval scientist Ibn al-Haytham and modern dictator Saddam Hussein. Choose one of these people and use the Internet or your school library to find out more about his or her life. Write a two-page biography of the person, and share it with your class.

This aerial view of a Baghdad suburb shows the clay brick houses, many with satellite dishes on the roofs for television reception. Baghdad is the largest city in Iraq, with a population of more than 7.2 million.

Communities

Traditionally Iraq was a country of small farming communities, but that changed during the second half of the 20th century. According to a 2011 study, 66.5 percent of Iraqis live in urban areas. The largest of these is Baghdad, the capital, with a population of approximately 7.2 million people. Other large cities in Iraq include Mosul (population estimated at around 1 million) and Basra (population: 1.5 million).

BAGHDAD

Baghdad was founded in CE 762 by Abu Jafar al-Mansur, the second Abbasid caliph. The city, originally built on the west bank of the Tigris River, was called Madinat as-Salam—"the City of Peace." Baghdad was the center of the Islamic world during the early decades of the Abbasid dynasty (750–1258), reaching its greatest level of prosperity in the ninth century.

The city was **sacked** by the Mongols during their 13th-century invasion. Though it was rebuilt, it would not regain its previous glory until the 1970s, as wealth from the sale of oil began to flow into Iraq.

Today, Baghdad sprawls across both banks of the Tigris River, covering an area of about 800 square miles (2,071 sq km). About one-quarter of Iraq's people live in or around the city. Much of Iraq's industry can be found near Baghdad. It is also the seat of government, as the Council of Representatives meets there and the president of Iraq has his office there.

Iraq contains many mosques and Islamic shrines dating back more than 1,000 years. Perhaps the most famous is the ninth-century Great Shrine of al-Mutawakkil, located outside Baghdad. Its spiral minaret soars 164 feet (50 meters). Another landmark near Baghdad is the Arch of Ctesiphon, which is all that is left of a Persian city built 2,200 years ago. The arch is believed to be the widest single-span brick vault in the world. The Baghdad Zoo is a popular tourist attraction, and Baghdad University is the second-largest university in the Arab world.

Unfortunately, in the past two decades life has grown harder for the residents of Baghdad. Allied bombing attacks during the 1991 Gulf War and the 2003 conflict turned large areas of the city into rubble. More recently, the city has been targeted by insurgents. In early 2015, a series of suicide bombings killed dozens of civilians. Baghdad is considered to be among the world's most dangerous

Words to Understand in This Chapter

sack—to capture, plunder, and destroy a city or town.
proximity—to be near or close to something else.

cities, and a 2011 study by an American consulting firm found that Baghdad had the worst quality of life of 221 major cities worldwide.

MOSUL

The second-largest city in Iraq is Mosul, located in the northern part of the country near the Kurdish region. For thousands of years Mosul has been known for textile exports. More recently, it served as an important center for oil refining, because it is near Iraq's northern oil fields, which are among the richest in the world.

In June 2014, the Islamic State captured Mosul from the Iraqi Army. It is the largest Iraqi city held by the Islamic State. The city had a population of about 1.8 million in 2008, but it is believed that more than half a million people fled Mosul after its capture. Most of them were Kurds, Shiite Muslims, or Christians, leaving Sunni Muslim Arabs as the predominant residents of Mosul. The Islamic State has maintained control of the city, although there have been problems like frequent power outages, as well as the execution without trial of many people that group deemed to be enemies. In January 2015, the United States launched airstrikes against Islamic State strongholds in Mosul, in support of a Kurdish effort to recapture the city.

 Did You Know?

The most famous Kurd in history was Saladin (1137–1193), who was born in the area that is now Iraq. Saladin was a great military leader who battled European armies during the Crusades, reconquering Jerusalem in 1187.

The city of Tikrit, located near Mosul, is notable as the birthplace of both the 12th-century Islamic leader Saladin and Saddam Hussein.

BASRA

Basra, in southeastern Iraq, is the country's principal port and one of its largest cities. It is located on the Shatt al Arab, about 75 miles

Shiite Muslims walk through the streets of An Najaf, Iraq. The city is considered sacred by Shiites, and is home to the mosque of Ali, one of the leaders of the early Muslim community.

(121 km) from the Persian Gulf. Basra is one of Iraq's oldest cities; it was founded in CE 636 by Caliph Umar I. It is located near an even older city—Ur, the ancient Sumerian city that flourished more than 4,000 years ago.

Because of Basra's ***proximity*** to southern Iraq's many oil fields, the city is an important center for petroleum production. Many refineries have been built in and around Basra.

Since the 1980s, control of the city has been heavily contested in Iraq's many conflicts, due to its strategic location on the Shatt al Arab near the Iran border. In 2014, Basra was supposed to host a a major international soccer tournament, the Gulf Cup of Nations, but the event had to be moved to Saudi Arabia because organizers were concerned that the athletes would not be safe there.

OTHER IMPORTANT CITIES

Erbil (population 1.5 million) is the capital of Iraqi Kurdistan. It is located 50 miles (81 km) east of Mosul. It is an important commercial center in the region. Erbil was founded thousands of years ago by the Medes. The city has grown significantly since 2003, thanks to generous foreign investment. An international airport was opened there in 2005, and companies like ExxonMobil and Chevron have operations in the region. Erbil is the center for government of the Kurdish region, and was defended by Kurdish soldiers, supported by U.S. airstrikes, in August 2014 when threatened by the forces of the Islamic State.

The Islamic State capture of Mosul also threatens Kirkuk (population 850,000), an important oil-producing center in northwestern Iraq. Kirkuk is connected via pipeline to the Mediterranean Sea. The city's origins date back about 5,000 years. Most of the inhabitants of Kirkuk are Kurds. Kurkuk is 90 miles (145 km) southeast of Mosul, and in late 2014 and early 2015 the city was subject to terrorist attacks launched by Islamic State guerrillas.

The two most important religious cities in Iraq are Karbala and An Najaf. Both are located in central Iraq. Karbala is the place where the Shiite leader Hussain ibn Ali was killed in battle in CE 680. A beautiful shrine in Karbala reminds Shiite pilgrims of Hussain's martyrdom. The tomb of Ali, the fourth Islamic caliph and the father of Hussain, is located in a mosque in nearby An Najaf. Shiite Muslims consider these two cities to be as important as Mecca and Medina.

Text-Dependent Questions

1. What city is the capital of Iraq? When was it built?
2. In what Iraqi city was the Medieval military leader Saladin born?
3. What are the most important religious cities in Iraq?

Research Project

The Battle of Karbala in 680 was a major event in the division of Muslim into Sunni and Shia sects. To understand why the city is revered today by Shiites, read the online article "Karbala: History's Long Shadow," from the BBC. It can be found at http://www.bbc.com/news/world-middle-east-22657029.

Two Iraqi boys pose beside a toppled statue of Saddam Hussein, April 14, 2003. Iraq's emergence from 24 years of ruthless rule under Saddam presented exciting possibilities—but also significant challenges.

Foreign Relations

In early April 2003, after just a few weeks of fighting, U.S. Marines helped a crowd of cheering Iraqis topple an enormous statue of Saddam Hussein in Baghdad. To many people around the world, this scene was a symbol of the toppling of Saddam Hussein's regime.

"Regime change" in Iraq had been a long-standing goal of President George W. Bush. Bush administration officials and their supporters expressed the hope that if Saddam's dictatorship fell, the United States could help build Iraq into a democracy—the first real democracy among the Arab states. And a successful, democratic Iraq, U.S. leaders said, might serve as a model for other Arab societies.

Things have not turned out the way the Bush administration hoped. Iraq has never really coalesced as a unified democratic state, and today a civil war is being fought along ethnic and religious lines.

Because of the leading role taken by the United States in Iraq's regime change, the U.S. remains deeply involved in Iraq's affairs. U.S. troops were stationed in Iraq from 2003 until December 2011. The United States has also provided financial assistance to the government of Iraq, and during 2014 sent military advisors to help the Iraqi government deal with the threat of ISIL.

IRAQ'S RELATIONS WITH IRAN

Although Iraq shares borders with both Iran and Turkey, the people of these three countries are separated by ethnicity, language, and culture. Throughout history, the area of modern-day Iraq was ruled by both Persian dynasties and by the Ottoman Empire. As a result, there remains some resentment toward Iraq's neighbors.

In 1979 strong-willed leaders came to power in both Iran and Iraq. Saddam Hussein had been one of the most powerful members of Iraq's Baath Party for more than a decade, but he seized total control of the government in a bloody purge. At the same time, in Iran, the government of Shah Mohammad Reza Pahlavi was being shaken. The shah, whose regime was supported by the United States, could not stop demonstrations and protests held throughout the country during much of 1978. When he fled Iran, a Shiite religious leader, Ayatollah Ruhollah Khomeini, seized power and established a theocratic state. The new Iranian government was very hostile toward the United States, which Khomeini called "the Great Satan."

Words to Understand in This Chapter

adversarial—a relationship that is characterized by conflict or opposition.

protectorate—a country that is defended by a more powerful state, which often exerts control over that country's foreign policy and relations.

President Barack Obama shakes hands with Iraqi Prime Minister Nouri al-Maliki during the U.S. leader's 2009 visit to Iraq.

The Iranian revolution posed a threat for Saddam Hussein and his secular dictatorship, particularly as Khomeini began to urge Shiites in other countries of the Middle East to rise up against their governments. Saddam feared that Iraq's majority Shiite population would join forces with Iran if the new theocracy were able to export its revolution.

There was a personal element as well. In 1964 Khomeini had been forced into exile from Iran; he settled in the Iraqi city of An Najaf, an important Shiite religious center. However, during the 1978 unrest in Iran, the shah asked the Iraqi government to expel Khomeini, who was inciting the public uprisings. Saddam was happy to get rid of Khomeini. However, he could not have been happy to see this enemy become the leader of a neighboring nation with more than twice as many people as Iraq.

Saddam Hussein may have decided to go to war with Iran in 1980 because the new Iranian government was not yet stable, and he hoped to weaken or destroy Khomeini's power. The Iran-Iraq War devastated both countries. After eight years of fighting, neither side had made significant territorial gains, and Iraq's economy had nearly been ruined. Yet after the two countries agreed to peace terms set by the United Nations, Saddam Hussein often boasted of his "victory" over Iran. However, the only reason the war might be considered a victory for Iraq is that Iran was weakened and its government lost the support of some of its people because of the sufferings caused by the war.

Iran strongly opposed the U.S. invasion of Iraq in 2003. However, relations between Iraq and Iran improved greatly after the fall of Saddam Hussein. Iraq began to permit Shia Muslims from Iran to make their traditional pilgrimage to Karbala, Najaf, and other holy sites in Iraq—a practice that had been outlawed during Saddam's regime. By 2005, the new Iraqi government and the Iranian regime had re-established diplomatic relations, and in 2008 Iranian president Mahmoud Ahmadinejad made a state visit to Iraq. Today, Iran is Iraq's largest trading partner, with their annual trade valued at more than $13 billion.

IRAQ'S RELATIONS WITH TURKEY

Both Iraq and Turkey have Kurdish minorities, and Turkish officials have long sought to prevent the two groups from joining together to create a separate Kurdish state. For decades, the Turks have struggled to suppress Kurdish nationalism, and during the 1990s Turkish troops occasionally entered northern Iraq, hunting for Kurdish rebels fighting against the Turkish government.

During the 1990s, Turkey's close ties to the United States and its membership in NATO meant that the country's relations with Iraq were generally **adversarial**. And in 1991, during the Gulf War,

Turkey closed an important oil pipeline that ran from Kirkuk to the Mediterranean Sea. That pipeline was reopened in 1997. Turkish airfields and other military facilities were used by U.S. warplanes patrolling the northern no-fly zone between 1991 and 2003.

Since the 1960s, Iraq has been concerned about Turkey's use of water from the Tigris and Euphrates Rivers. Hydroelectric dams on those rivers in Turkey greatly affect the amount of water that flows into Iraq. In 2008, the Iraqi government successfully petitioned Turkey to release additional water in order to combat a drought. Nonetheless, water rights continue to be an issue between the two countries.

In 2003, the Turkish parliament voted against participating in the U.S.-led invasion of Iraq. This was in large part due to its concern about the Kurdish population of northern Iraq, and fears that if the state broke apart Iraqi Kurdistan would become an independent country—which, Turkish leaders feared, would encourage the Kurdish population in Turkey to seek to break away and become part of Kurdistan.

Since the fall of Saddam Hussein, Turkey has attempted to work with all of the factions in Iraq—Shiite and Sunni Arabs, as well as Kurds—in hopes of keeping the country together and preventing an independent Kurdistan. Relations between Turkey and the semi-autonomous government of Iraqi Kurdistan have grown warmer in recent years. However, one area where there has been tension concerns the Kurdistan Workers' Party (PKK), an organization of Kurds that have been fighting for freedom from Turkey for decades. Many countries, including the United States, Turkey, and Iraq, consider the PKK a terrorist organization. Nonetheless, PKK fighters have hidden in the Zagros Mountains of Iraqi Kurdistan, and occasionally launched attacks from that region against Turkish targets. In response, the Turkish military has occasionally invaded the border regions in an attempt to stamp out the PKK in that region.

IRAQ AND THE ARAB WORLD

Until the Gulf War, Iraq was a major force in the region mainly because of its military strength—as of 1991 it had the fourth-largest army in the entire world, with nearly one million active-duty soldiers. At various times Iraqi military strength has alarmed its Arab neighbors—Kuwait, Saudi Arabia, Jordan, and Syria—as some of Iraq's leaders have clearly indicated their desire to rule over a united Arab nation.

Historically, Iraqi leaders have considered Kuwait to be part of their territory. The tiny kingdom of Kuwait was founded in 1756. Although it was on the fringes of the Ottoman Empire in the 18th and 19th centuries, it was never really part of the empire. British influence was more prevalent than Turkish; in 1899 Kuwait became a British *protectorate*, and remained under British control until 1961, when it became an independent state.

Long before Iraq's 1990 invasion of Kuwait, the leaders of Iraq coveted Kuwait's oil wealth as well as its long coastline on the Persian Gulf. As early as 1940, King Ghazi of Iraq talked about making Kuwait part of his country. Later, when Abd al-Karim Qasim took over the reins of government in 1961, he claimed Kuwait for Iraq and threatened to invade—an invasion that was cancelled only after British warships and troops were rushed to the Gulf to protect Kuwait. When the Baath Party came to power in Iraq in 1963, it recognized the independence of Kuwait; a few years later, however, the Baath Party began to pressure Kuwait to become part of Iraq.

During the Iran-Iraq War, the government of Kuwait loaned $10 billion to Iraq. After the war had ended, however, Saddam Hussein said that Kuwait should consider the money a grant rather than a loan. Saddam's argument was that Iraq had protected Kuwait and the other Arab nations by fighting with Iran—an assertion that failed to convince many in the Arab world. Kuwait's refusal to write off the debt was one of the reasons Iraq invaded the country in August 1990.

After the Gulf War, the two Arab countries attempted to improve their frayed relations. In November 1994, Iraq gave up its claim to Kuwait and to the Bubiyan and Warbah islands when it formally accepted borders established by the United Nations. And in March 2002, Iraq signed an agreement with Kuwait in which it promised to respect the country's sovereignty. This agreement, negotiated through the diplomatic efforts of Qatar and Oman, occurred at an Arab League summit in Lebanon. Since the fall of Saddam Hussein's government, Iraq and Kuwait have re-established normal relations.

Iraq's relationship with Saudi Arabia has also undergone many changes. In the early 1970s, Iraq's leaders sometimes spoke out against the ruling family of Saudi Arabia. But in the years before Saddam Hussein seized total power, he began to cultivate a better relationship with the Saudis. When Saddam became president of Iraq, the Saudi government supported him, and when Iraq started its war against Iran in 1980, the Saudis were willing to provide financial assistance. Eventually, Saudi Arabia loaned Iraq almost $26 billion. However, when the war finally ended in 1988, Saddam refused to repay the loan, insisting—as he had with Kuwait—that it should be considered a grant, because Iraq had protected the Arab Gulf states from the danger of Iranian aggression.

After Saddam invaded Kuwait, Saudi Arabia's leaders feared their country would be next. The Saudi monarchy publicly opposed Iraq's occupation of Kuwait and permitted the international coalition to use bases on Saudi soil. Saudi Arabia was a key member of the coalition. More than half a million soldiers were assembled on Saudi territory, and the attack on Iraq came from Saudi Arabia. The government also shut down an oil pipeline from Iraq that had been built in 1985, a move that constricted Iraq's economy.

Relations between Saudi Arabia and Iraq remained uneasy after the end of the 1991 Gulf War. However, when the United States was making its preparations to attack Iraq in late 2002 and early 2003, the Saudis refused to allow bases in their country to be used for the war against Saddam Hussein's regime. Saudi leaders feared that the country would fracture along religious and ethnic lines—a belief that turned out to be correct. In 2012 Saudi Arabia sent an ambassador to Iraq for the first time since 1990.

Jordan was one of the few countries that did not condemn Iraq's 1990 invasion of Kuwait. Jordan's King Hussein made this decision in part because of fears about the stability of his own government. Jordan, which also borders Israel, has a large population of Palestinian Arabs. The Palestinians overwhelmingly supported Saddam Hussein, and the king was concerned that they might revolt and overthrow his monarchy if he joined the U.S.-led coalition against Iraq.

Because Jordan is small, it has tried to maintain good relations with all of its neighbors. While Iraq was under international sanctions, Jordan received lucrative contracts to provide food in exchange for Iraqi oil. Jordan was also one of the first Arab states to establish normal relations with the new Iraqi government after the 2003 invasion. The two countries have conducted a lucrative trade since then, although the 2014 capture of territory in Anbar province by ISIL has affected this trade. ISIL imposes a high tax on all trucks carrying goods through the province.

The relationship between Syria and Iraq is very complicated. Although both were ruled for many years by the Baath Party, the Syrian and Iraqi governments tended to be rivals, with each believing its version of Baath philosophy to be the correct one. Syria's support of Iran during its 1980-88 war against Iraq added to the hostility, and its participation in the U.S.-led coalition that drove Iraq out of Kuwait in the 1991 Gulf War further damaged Syrian-Iraqi relations. The two countries have frequently battled over the water rights of the Euphrates, as well as the management of the oil pipeline running from Iraq through Syria.

Despite this rivalry, Syria strongly opposed the 2003 invasion of Iraq by U.S. forces. The invasion ended Baath Party rule in Iraq, overthrowing the regime of Saddam Hussein. It also created a surge of millions of Iraqi refugees who crossed the border into Syria.

During the 2000s, as the U.S. military occupied Iraq and attempted to rebuild the state, the Syrian government was often accused of permitting terrorists to cross the Syrian border and enter Iraq, where they could sow discord and violence. After the Syrian civil war began in 2011, armed fighters from Iraq crossed the border to join anti-government rebel groups. By 2014 the Islamist organization Islamic State of Iraq and the Levant (ISIL) had seized territory in both Iraq and Syria, where it collected taxes and enforced its version of Sharia laws, including draconian punishments such as the public execution of those considered to be unfaithful to Sunni Muslim principles, such as Iraqi Christians and Shiite Muslims.

 ## Text-Dependent Questions

1. How has Iraq's relationship with Iran changed over the past decade?
2. What is the Iraqi government's current attitude toward Kuwait? Does it still claim the territory as part of Iraq?
3. What 2014 event has negatively affected trade between Iraq and Jordan?

 ## Research Project

In Islam, a caliphate is a theocratic state in which the ruler (known as a caliph), has authority over both the spiritual and temporal lives of his subjects and all people must obey Islamic laws. The organization ISIL has declared that it is forming a new caliphate, to which all Muslims must pledge allegiance. Find a world map online, and identify the ten countries with the greatest population of Muslims (Indonesia, Pakistan, India, Bangladesh, Egypt, Nigeria, Iran, Turkey, Algeria, and Morocco. How close are these countries to the lands where ISIL holds territory (Iraq and Syria)?

CHRONOLOGY

9000 bce: Earliest settlements established in the mountains of northeast Iraq.

ca. 3000 BCE: Sumer flourishes in southern Iraq.

ca. 1750 BCE: Hammurabi, who becomes famous for his code of laws, rules in Babylon.

1150 BCE: Assyria conquers Babylon.

612 BCE: The Assyrian Empire, with its capital at Nineveh in central Iraq, is conquered by Babylonian armies under Nebuchadnezzar.

539 BCE: Babylon falls to the Persians under Cyrus the Great.

331 BCE: The armies of Alexander the Great conquer the Persians and take control of Mesopotamia.

126 BCE: Parthians, invaders from northern Persia, conquer Mesopotamia.

ca. CE 570: Muhammad, founder of the Islamic faith, is born in Mecca in the Arabian Peninsula.

636:   Arabs defeat the Persians and conquer Iraq.

680:   Hussein, grandson of Muhammad, is martyred in Karbala.

762:   Baghdad is built as the capital of the Arab Muslim empire.

1258:   Mongols capture Baghdad.

1453:   Ottoman Turks conquer Constantinople, bringing an end to the Byzantine Empire.

1530:   Ottoman armies conquer Baghdad and bring Mesopotamia into the Ottoman Empire.

1914:   The Ottomans ally with Germany and Austria-Hungary during the First World War; British forces occupy Basra, in southern Iraq.

1917:   British armies occupy Baghdad.

1918:   The First World War ends.

1920:   League of Nations gives British a mandate to administer Iraq.

1921:   A monarchy, ruled by the Hashemite King Faisal I, is established in Iraq.

1927:   Oil discovered at Kirkuk, in northern Iraq.

1932:   British mandate ends, and Iraq becomes independent.

1933:   King Faisal dies; his son Ghazi becomes king.

1939:   King Ghazi dies in a car accident; Abdulillah rules Iraq as regent until Ghazi's infant son Faisal II is old enough to rule.

CHRONOLOGY

1953:   King Faisal II crowned.

1958:   Revolution takes place on July 13, and Abd al-Karim Qasim becomes the new ruler of Iraq.

1963:   Qasim is killed after a coup by the Baath Party, but when Abd al-Salam Arif becomes president, he puts the Baathists out of power.

1966:   Arif dies in helicopter crash; brother Abd al-Rahman Arif becomes president.

1967:   Iraqi troops are sent to Jordan during the June 1967 war with Israel.

1968:   After a military coup orchestrated by the Baath Party, Ahmad Hasan al-Bakr becomes president and exiles Abd al-Rahman Arif.

1969:   Saddam Hussein becomes vice-chairman of the Revolutionary Command Council.

1978:   The Iranian Shiite cleric Ayatollah Ruhollah Khomeini is expelled from Iraq.

1979:   In July, Saddam Hussein becomes president of Iraq after a purge of the Revolutionary Command Council.

1980:   In September, Iraq attacks Iran, beginning an eight-year-long war.

1988:   The United Nations brokers a cease-fire to end the Iran-Iraq War.

1990:   Iraq invades Kuwait, announcing that it has annexed the tiny kingdom; the international community pressures Iraq to withdraw and places sanctions on the country.

1991:   An international coalition forces Iraq to withdraw from Kuwait in the brief Gulf War; the United Nations Security Council passes resolutions demanding that Iraq disarm and eliminate its programs to develop chemical, biological, and nuclear weapons.

1998:   After a year of crises over the weapons inspectors, the United States launches a cruise missile attack against Iraq.

2002:   George W. Bush declares Iraq part of an "axis of evil," along with Iran and North Korea; U.N. weapons inspectors return to Iraq.

2003:   The U.N. pulls inspectors out of Iraq at the suggestion of the United States; the United States and Great Britain invade Iraq in March, toppling the regime of Saddam Hussein; on July 22 Saddam's sons Qusay and Uday are killed by soldiers of the U.S. Army's 101st Airborne Division; Saddam Hussein is captured on December 13 by soldiers from the Fourth Infantry Division.

CHRONOLOGY

2004:   The Coalition Provisional Authority is scheduled to hand over power to an Iraqi provisional government by the end of June.

2005:   The Shia-dominated United Iraqi Alliance wins a majority of seats in the historic parliamentary election held January 30; efforts to involve Sunni Muslims slow down the formation of Iraq's new government under Prime Minister Ibrahim Jaafari. In October, Iraqis approve a new constitution that creates an Islamic federal system of government. In December, Iraqi voters select members of a permanent parliament.

2006:   In February an important Shiite shrine, the Golden Mosque of Samarra, is bombed, igniting a wave of sectarian killings. After months of political stalemate, the leader of the Shiite Dawa Party, Nouri al-Maliki, is asked to form a government. In November Saddam Hussein is found guilty of crimes against humanity; he is executed in December.

2007:   President Bush announces an American troop "surge"; the Sunni Awakening, which began in Anbar Province, begins to spread. In August Moqtada al-Sadr, head of the Mehdi Army, a powerful Shiite militia, announces a cease-fire. Violence in Iraq begins to subside by the end of the year.

2008:   In March Prime Minister Maliki orders a crackdown on the Mehdi Army in Basra. In November the Iraqi parliament approves an agreement by which American troops are to leave Iraq by the end of 2011.

2009:   Candidates allied with Prime Minister Maliki do very well in provincial elections in February. In June, U.S. troops begin to withdraw from Iraqi cities and villages. Throughout the year, a terrorist group linked to al-Qaeda that calls itself the Islamic State of Iraq carries out suicide bombings in Baghdad and other cities that kill approximately 400 people.

2010:   In January, Ali Hassan al-Majid, a key figure in Saddam Hussein's government who was nicknamed Chemical Ali" for his use of chemical weapons against Iraq's Kurdish population during the 1980s, is executed. In August, the last U.S. combat brigade leaves Iraq. In October, more than 50 Iraqi Christians are massacred by militants in Baghdad. In December, the COuncil of Representatives re-appoints Jalal Talabani as president and Nouri al-Maliki as prime minister.

2011:   In December, the United States withdraws the last of its troops from Iraq.

2012:   Terrorist attacks targeting Shia Muslims spark fears of a new sectarian conflict. Nearly 200 people are killed in January, more than 160 in June, 113 in a single day in July, more than 70 people in August, about 62 in attacks nation-wide in September, and at least 35 before and during the Shia mourning month of Muharram in November. Thousands of Syrians flee to neighboring countries, including Iraq, to escape the civil war in that country.

2013: The insurgency in Iraq intensifies, and by June experts agree that the situation has become a civil war. The United Nations estimates that 7,157 civilians were killed during 2013, a significant increase over the 2012 figure of 3,238.

2014: Islamist fighters infiltrate Fallujah and Ramadi after months of mounting violence in mainly-Sunni Anbar province. Government forces recapture Ramadi but face entrenched rebels in Fallujah. In June, the Islamic State of Iraq and the Levant (ISIL) seizes Mosul and other key towns. Kurdish forces assist the Iraqi military in repelling attacks, with assistance from Iran and the United States.

2015: In January, terrorist bombings in Baghdad and Kirkuk, carried out by ISIL guerrillas, kill dozens of people. A U.S.-led military coalition continues to launch airstrikes against the Islamic State of Iraq and the Levant in support of Iraqi and Kurdish efforts to recapture Mosul. In May, ISIL gains control of the city of Ramadi, the capital of Anbar province.

SERIES GLOSSARY

autonomy—the right of self-government.

BCE and CE—an alternative to the traditional Western designation of calendar eras, which used the birth of Jesus as a dividing line. BCE stands for "Before the Common Era," and is equivalent to BC ("Before Christ"). Dates labeled CE, or "Common Era," are equivalent to Anno Domini (AD, or "the Year of Our Lord").

caliphate—an Islamic theocratic state, in which the ruler, or caliph, has authority over both the spiritual and temporal lives of his subjects and all people must obey Islamic laws.

civil society—the sum total of institutions, organizations, and groups promoting social and civic causes in a country (for example, human rights groups, labor unions, arts foundations) that are not funded or controlled by the government or business interests.

colonialism—control or domination by one country over an area or people outside its boundaries; the policy of colonizing foreign lands.

ideology—a system of beliefs, values, and ideas forming the basis of a social, economic, or political philosophy.

Islamist—a Muslim who advocates the reformation of society and government in accordance with Islamic laws and principles.

jihadism—adherence to the idea that Muslims should carry out a war against un-Islamic groups and ideas, especially Westerners and Western liberal culture.

nationalism—the belief that shared ethnicity, language, and history should form the basis for political organization; the desire of people with a common culture to have their own state.

Pan-Arabism—a movement seeking to unite all Arab peoples into a single state.

self-determination—determination by a people of their own future political status.

Sharia—Islamic law, based on the Qur'an and other Islamic writings and traditions. The Sharia sets forth the moral goals of an Islamic society, and governs a Muslim's religious political, social, and private life.

Shia—the smaller of Islam's two major branches, whose rift with the larger Sunni branch originated in seventh-century disputes over who should succeed the prophet Muhammad as leader of the Muslim community.

Sunni—a Muslim who belongs to the largest branch of Islam.

Wahhabism—a highly conservative form of Sunni Islam practiced in Saudi Arabia.

Zionism—the movement to establish a Jewish state in Palestine; support for the State of Israel.

FURTHER READING

Arnold, James R. *Saddam Hussein's Iraq.* Brookfield, Conn.: Twenty-First Century Books, 2008.

Cockburn, Andrew, and Peter Cockburn. *Out of the Ashes: The Resurrection of Saddam Hussein.* New York: HarperCollins, 1999.

Fernea, Elizabeth Warnock, and Robert A. Fernea. *The Arab World: Forty Years of Change.* New York: Bantam Doubleday Dell, 1997.

Field, Michael. *Inside the Arab World.* Cambridge, Mass.: Harvard University Press, 1995.

Gallagher, Jim. *Causes of the Iraq War.* Stockton, N.J.: OTTN Publishing, 2006.

Haass, Richard N. *War of Necessity: A Memoir of Two Iraq Wars.* New York: Simon and Schuster, 2009.

Hiro, Dilip. *Neighbors, Not Friends: Iraq and Iran After the Gulf Wars.* New York: Routledge, 2001.

Joffe, George. *A Century of Arab Revolution: The Legacy of Empires.* London: I.B. Tauris, 2015.

Mackey, Sandra. *The Reckoning: Iraq and the Legacy of Saddam Hussein.* New York: W. W. Norton, 2002.

Mansfield, Peter. *A History of the Middle East.* 4th ed. revised and updated by Nicholas Pelham. New York: Penguin Books, 2013.

Ricks, Thomas E. *The Gamble: General David Petraeus and the American Military Adventure in Iraq, 2006-2008.* New York: Penguin Press, 2009.

Sekulow, Jay. *Rise of ISIS: A Threat We Can't Ignore.* New York: Howard Books, 2014.

Stern, Jessica, and J.M. Berger. *ISIS: The State of Terror.* New York: Ecco, 2015.

Tripp, Charles. *A History of Iraq.* Cambridge, UK: Cambridge University Press, 2000.

Wagner, Heather Lehr. *Iraq.* New York: Chelsea House, 2008.

West, Bing. *The Strongest Tribe: War, Politics, and the Endgame in Iraq.* New York: Random House, 2008.

Woodward, Bob. *The War Within: A Secret White House History, 2006-2008.* New York: Simon and Schuster, 2008.

Wien, Peter. *Arab Nationalism: The Politics of History and Culture in the Modern Middle East.* New York: Routledge, 2015.

http://travel.state.gov/travel/cis_pa_tw/cis/cis_1144.html

Information about Iraq, including links to informative articles, provided by the U.S. State Department.

www.cia.gov/library/publications/the-world-factbook/geos/iz.html

The CIA World Factbook website provides a great deal of statistical information about Iraq and its people. It is regularly updated.

www.un.org/english

The English-language web page for the United Nations can be searched for Iraq-related stories and information.

http://iraq.usembassy.gov

The website of the U.S. embassy in Iraq includes news stories and photographs about the country, as well as about American activities and programs there.

www.bbc.com/news

The official website of BBC News provides articles and videos on important international news and events related to the Middle East and elsewhere.

www.aljazeera.com

The English-language website of the Arabic news service Al Jazeera provides articles and videos on breaking news, as well as feature stories that provide background material, including profiles of leaders and essays reacting to major events.

www.fpri.org

The website of the Foreign Policy Research Institute includes informative essays by FPRI scholars on events in the Middle East.

INDEX

Numbers in **bold italic** refer to captions.

INDEX

PICTURE CREDITS

CONTRIBUTORS

Senior Consultant CAMILLE PECASTAING, PH.D., is acting director of the Middle East Studies Program at the Paul H. Nitze School of Advanced International Studies at Johns Hopkins University. A student of behavioral sciences and historical sociology, Dr. Pecastaing's research focuses on the cognitive and emotive foundations of xenophobic political cultures and ethnoreligious violence, using the Muslim world and its European and Asian peripheries as a case study. He has written on political Islam, Islamist terrorism, social change, and globalization. Pecastaing's essays have appeared in many journals, including *World Affairs* and *Policy Review*. He is the author of *Jihad in the Arabian Sea* (Hoover Institution Press, 2011).

The FOREIGN POLICY RESEARCH INSTITUTE (FPRI) served as editorial consultants for this series. FPRI is one of the nation's oldest "think tanks." The Institute's Middle East Program focuses on Gulf security, monitors the Arab-Israeli peace process, and sponsors an annual conference for teachers on the Middle East, plus periodic briefings on key developments in the region.

Among FPRI's trustees are a former Undersecretary of Defense, a former Secretary of the Navy, a former Assistant Secretary of State, a foundation president, and numerous active or retired corporate CEOs, lawyers, and civic leaders. Scholars affiliated with FPRI include a Pulitzer Prize–winning historian; a former president of Swarthmore College; a Bancroft Prize–winning historian; and a former Ambassador and senior staff member of the National Security Council. And FPRI counts among its extended network of scholars—especially its Inter-University Study Groups—representatives of many diverse disciplines, including political science, history, economics, law, management, religion, sociology, and psychology.

BILL THOMPSON graduated from Boston University with a degree in education. After teaching history in public schools, Mr. Thompson earned a Master of Divinity from Colgate-Rochester and became a Presbyterian minister. He pastored in New York, New Jersey, and Florida. He and his wife, Dorcas, now live in Swarthmore, Pennsylvania. DORCAS (BOARDMAN) THOMPSON graduated from Wheaton College in Illinois with a bachelor's degree in history. She taught history and social studies in Massachusetts and Pennsylvania. She has served as librarian in a private school and worked as an editor for an educational publisher in Massachusetts. She was named to *Who's Who Among America's Teachers* in 1992. The Thompsons have one daughter, Rebecca Mandia, who lives in Pennsylvania with her teacher-husband, Al. Bill and Dorcas have two grandchildren, Rachel and Patrick.